D. H. LAWRENCE

EDITED AND WITH AN
INTRODUCTION BY HAROLD BLOOM

CURRENTLY AVAILABLE

BLOOM'S MAJOR DRAMATISTS

Aeschylus
Anton Chekhov
Aristophanes
Berthold Brecht
Euripides
Henrik Ibsen
Ben Jonson
Christopher Marlowe
Arthur Miller
Eugene O'Neill
Shakespeare's Comedies
Shakespeare's Histories
Shakespeare's Romances
Shakespeare's Tragedies
George Bernard Shaw
Neil Simon
Sophocles
Tennessee Williams
August Wilson

BLOOM'S MAJOR NOVELISTS

Jane Austen
The Brontës
Willa Cather
Stephen Crane
Charles Dickens
Fyodor Dostoevsky
William Faulkner
F. Scott Fitzgerald
Thomas Hardy
Nathaniel Hawthorne
Ernest Hemingway
Henry James
James Joyce
D. H. Lawrence
Toni Morrison
John Steinbeck
Stendhal
Leo Tolstoy
Mark Twain
Alice Walker
Edith Wharton
Virginia Woolf

BLOOM'S MAJOR WORLD POETS

Geoffrey Chaucer
Emily Dickinson
John Donne
T. S. Eliot
Robert Frost
Langston Hughes
John Milton
Edgar Allan Poe
Shakespeare's Poems & Sonnets
Alfred, Lord Tennyson
Walt Whitman
William Wordsworth

BLOOM'S MAJOR SHORT STORY WRITERS

William Faulkner
F. Scott Fitzgerald
Ernest Hemingway
O. Henry
James Joyce
Herman Melville
Flannery O'Connor
Edgar Allan Poe
J. D. Salinger
John Steinbeck
Mark Twain
Eudora Welty

D. H. LAWRENCE

EDITED AND WITH AN INTRODUCTION
BY HAROLD BLOOM

© 2002 by Chelsea House Publishers, a subsidiary of
Haights Cross Communications.

Introduction © 2002 by Harold Bloom.

All rights reserved. No part of this publication may be reproduced
or transmitted in any form or by any means without the written
permission of the publisher.

Printed and bound in the United States of America.

First Printing
1 3 5 7 9 8 6 4 2

Library of Congress Cataloging-in-Publication Data
D. H. Lawrence / edited and with an introduction by Harold Bloom.
      p. cm.—(Bloom's major novelists)
   Includes bibliographical references and index.
   ISBN 0-7910-6350-X (alk. paper)
  1. Lawrence, D. H. (David Herbert), 1885–1930—Criticism and
interpretation. I. Bloom, Harold. II. Series.

PR6023.A93 Z62337 2001b
823'.912—dc21   2001047590

Chelsea House Publishers
1974 Sproul Road, Suite 400
Broomall, PA 19008-0914

The Chelsea House World Wide Web address is
http://www.chelseahouse.com

Series Editor: Matt Uhler

Contributing Editor: Elizabeth Beaudin

Produced by Publisher's Services, Santa Barbara, California

Contents

User's Guide	7
Editor's Note	8
Introduction	9
Biography of D. H. Lawrence	13
Plot Summary of *Sons and Lovers*	16
List of Characters in *Sons and Lovers*	21
Critical Views on *Sons and Lovers*	
Letter from D. H. Lawrence to Edward Garnett	23
Judith Arcana on Mother-Blaming in *Sons and Lovers*	25
Helen Baron on Lawrence's *Sons and Lovers* versus Garnett's	27
Helen Baron on Disseminated Consciousness	29
Gerald Doherty on the Dialectic of Space	32
Adrienne E. Gavin on the Labeling of Miriam Leivers	34
Robert Kiely on the Language and Power of the Working Class	36
Margaret Storch on Images of Women in Lawrence	38
Plot Summary of *The Rainbow*	41
List of Characters in *The Rainbow*	46
Critical Views on *The Rainbow*	
Letter from D. H. Lawrence to Lady Ottoline Morrell	48
Letter from D. H. Lawrence to J. B. Pinker	49
Diane S. Bonds on D. H. Lawrence's Literary Inheritors	50
Elaine Feinstein on Lawrence's Women	52
Mark Kinkead-Weekes on the Exploratory Imagination of D. H. Lawrence	55
Henry Miller on the World of Lawrence	58
Paul Poplawski on Creativity and the Religious Impulse	60
Jack Stewart on Vision and Expression	63
Plot Summary of *Women in Love*	66
List of Characters in *Women in Love*	72
Critical Views on *Women in Love*	
Letter from D. H. Lawrence to J. B. Pinker	74
Gerald Doherty on Death and the Rhetoric of Representation	75
Earl Ingersoll on Staging the Gaze	77

Eric P. Levy on Lawrence's Psychology of Void and Center	82
Norman Mailer on the Prisoner of Sex	83
David Parker on the Ideological Unknown	86
John Worthen on the First *Women in Love*	91
Plot Summary of *Lady Chatterley's Lover*	95
List of Characters in *Lady Chatterley's Lover*	102
Critical Views on *Lady Chatterley's Lover*	
Letter from D. H. Lawrence to Nelly Morrison	104
Carl Bedient on the Radicalism of *Lady Chatterley's Lover*	105
Charles M. Burack on the Assault on Verbal and Visual Consciousness	107
John B. Humma on Metaphor and Meaning	110
Aldous Huxley on D. H. Lawrence	112
Barry J. Scherr on Lawrentian *Daemonization* and *Askesis*	114
Carol Siegel on Lawrence's Responses to His Female Precursors	116
Stanley Sultan on Lawrence the Anti-Autobiographer	120
Works by D. H. Lawrence	122
Works About D. H. Lawrence	123
Index of Themes and Ideas	126

User's Guide

This volume is designed to present biographical, critical, and bibliographical information on the author's best-known or most important works. Following Harold Bloom's editor's note and introduction is a detailed biography of the author, discussing major life events and important literary accomplishments. A plot summary of each novel follows, tracing significant themes, patterns, and motifs in the work.

A selection of critical extracts, derived from previously published material from leading critics, analyzes aspects of each work. The extracts consist of statements from the author, if available, early reviews of the work, and later evaluations up to the present. A bibliography of the author's writings (including a complete list of all works written, cowritten, edited, and translated), a list of additional books and articles on the author and his or her work, and an index of themes and ideas in the author's writings conclude the volume.

Harold Bloom is Sterling Professor of the Humanities at Yale University and Henry W. and Albert A. Berg Professor of English at the New York University Graduate School. He is the author of over 20 books, including *Shelley's Mythmaking* (1959), *The Visionary Company* (1961), *Blake's Apocalypse* (1963), *Yeats* (1970), *A Map of Misreading* (1975), *Kabbalah and Criticism* (1975), *Agon: Toward a Theory of Revisionism* (1982), *The American Religion* (1992), *The Western Canon* (1994), and *Omens of Millennium: The Gnosis of Angels, Dreams, and Resurrection* (1996). *The Anxiety of Influence* (1973) sets forth Professor Bloom's provocative theory of the literary relationships between the great writers and their predecessors. His most recent books include *Shakespeare: The Invention of the Human,* a 1998 National Book Award finalist, and *How to Read and Why,* which was published in 2000.

Professor Bloom earned his Ph.D. from Yale University in 1955 and has served on the Yale faculty since then. He is a 1985 MacArthur Foundation Award recipient, served as the Charles Eliot Norton Professor of Poetry at Harvard University in 1987–88, and has received honorary degrees from the universities of Rome and Bologna. In 1999, Professor Bloom received the prestigious American Academy of Arts and Letters Gold Medal for Criticism.

Currently, Harold Bloom is the editor of numerous Chelsea House volumes of literary criticism, including the series BLOOM'S NOTES, BLOOM'S MAJOR DRAMATISTS, BLOOM'S MAJOR NOVELISTS, MAJOR LITERARY CHARACTERS, MODERN CRITICAL VIEWS, MODERN CRITICAL INTERPRETATIONS, and WOMEN WRITERS OF ENGLISH AND THEIR WORKS.

Editor's Note

My Introduction centers upon Lawrence's largest achievement, the double-novel, *The Rainbow* and *Women in Love*, emphasizing Lawrence's mastery of erotic strife.

Each of the four parts of this little volume begins with crucial letters from Lawrence himself. As there are more than twenty-five critical excerpts, all highly useful, I will comment briefly only upon a few I find particularly relevant to my own views of Lawrence.

Sons and Lovers, which is Lawrence's *Portrait of the Artist as a Young Man,* is exonerated by Judith Arcana from the usual charge of mother-blaming, while Helen Baron, the textual editor of the best edition of the novel, defends Lawrence against his first editor, Edward Garnett, and then gives an instance of Garnett's mal-editing. Robert Kiely comments upon Lawrence's deliberate use of working-class idiom, after which Margaret Storch chronicles a striking instance of Paul's sadistic fantasy directed against his mother.

Mark Kinkead-Weekes explores the relationships between Lawrence's *Study of Thomas Hardy* and *The Rainbow,* while the novelist Henry Miller, praising Lawrence as a "superb chaos," sees the author of *The Rainbow* as glorifying woman in order to punish her.

Norman Mailer, whose affinities to Henry Miller are palpably omnipresent, famously terms Lawrence "the prisoner of sex," after which both David Parker and John Worthen expertly analyze different aspects of *Women in Love.*

"Sex in the head," a horror to Lawrence, is studied by Charles M. Burack as Lawrence's target in his readers' consciousness, more intensely in *Lady Chatterley's Lover* than even before.

John B. Humma insightfully meditates upon Lawrence's nature metaphors, while the novelist-essayist Aldous Huxley, a good friend to Lawrence, comments upon the sadness of *Lady Chatterley's Lover* as a reflection of the melancholy of Lawrence's life.

The indubitable influence of the Brontë sisters, who taught Lawrence how to represent female anger, is demonstrated by Carol Siegel, after which Stanley Sultan gently deprecates the general view that Lawrence's fictions are directly autobiographical.

Introduction

HAROLD BLOOM

Lawrence's greatest achievement is his double-novel, *The Rainbow* (1915) and *Women in Love* (1920). Together with his short stories and the best of his poems, these represent his absolute literary permanence, obscured as that currently may be by the virulence of much Feminist criticism.

I recall, many years ago, writing that: "In the endless war between men and women, Lawrence fights on both sides." The twenty-third chapter of *Women in Love,* "Excurse," is an eminent instance:

> "I jealous! *I*—jealous! You *are* mistaken if you think that. I'm not jealous in the least of Hermione, she is nothing to me, not *that*!" And Ursula snapped her fingers. "No, it's you who are a liar. It's you who must return, like a dog to his vomit. It is what Hermione *stands* for that *I hate*. I *hate* it. It is lies, it is false, it is death. But you want to, you can't help it, you can't help yourself. You belong to that old, deathly way of living—then go back to it. But don't come to me, for I've nothing to do with it."
>
> And in the stress of her violent emotion, she got down from the car and went to the hedgerow, picking unconsciously some flesh-pink spindleberries, some of which were burst, showing their orange seeds.
>
> "Ah, you are a fool," he cried bitterly, with some contempt.
>
> "Yes, I am. I *am* a fool. And thank God for it. I'm too big a fool to swallow your cleverness. God be praised. You go to your women—go to them—they are your sort—you've always had a string of them trailing after you—and you always will. Go to your spiritual brides—but don't come to me as well, because I'm not having any, thank you. You're not satisfied, are you? Your spiritual brides can't give you what you want, they aren't common and fleshy enough for you, aren't they? So you come to me, and keep them in the background! You will marry me for daily use. But you'll keep yourself well provided with spiritual brides in the background. I know your dirty little game." Suddenly a flame ran over her, and she stamped her foot madly on the

road, and he winced, afraid she would strike him. "And *I, I'm* not spiritual enough. *I'm* not as spiritual as that Hermione—!" Her brows knitted, her eyes blazed like a tiger's. "Then *go* to her, that's all I say, *go* to her, *go*. Ha, she spiritual—*spiritual,* she! A dirty materialist as she is. *She* spiritual? What does she care for, what is her spirituality? What *is* it?" Her fury seemed to blaze out and burn his face. He shrank a little. "I tell you, it's *dirt, dirt,* and nothing *but* dirt. And it's dirt you want, you crave for it. Spiritual! Is *that* spiritual, her bullying, her conceit, her sordid materialism? She's a fishwife, a fishwife, she is such a materialist. And all so sordid. What does she work out to, in the end, with all her social passion, as you call it. Social passion—what social passion has she?—show it me!—where is it? She wants petty, immediate *power,* she wants the illusion that she is a great woman, that is all. In her soul she's a devilish unbeliever, common as dirt. That's what she is, at the bottom. And all the rest is pretence—but you love it. You love the sham spiritually, it's your food. And why? Because of the dirt underneath. Do you think I don't know the foulness of your sex life—and hers?—I do. And it's that foulness you want, you liar. Then have it, have it. You're such a liar."

She turned away, spasmodically tearing the twigs of spindleberry from the hedge, and fastening them, with vibrating fingers, in the bosom of her coat.

He stood watching in silence. A wonderful tenderness burned in him at the sight of her quivering, so sensitive fingers: and at the same time he was full of rage and callousness.

The ambivalence of the lovers, so memorably rendered, reflects not only Lawrence's stormy marriage with Frieda, but his own repressed bisexuality as well. And yet the passage matters aesthetically because of the marvelous detail, at once literal and metaphoric, or Ursula's tearing of the spindleberries, flesh-like and bursting with life. Lawrence had the rare gift, inherited from Charlotte Brontë and Thomas Hardy, of portraying a woman's anger with total sympathy and virtual identification. Since Birkin is a deliberate parody of the prophetic Lawrence, fiercely exalting yet also recoiling from sexual love, Ursula's fury is accurate and precise.

After Shakespeare and Tolstoy, no writer expresses more vividly than Lawrence the perpetually prevalent male ambivalence towards female superiority in natural sexuality. A powerful example in Lawrence is the farewell love-making between Ursula and Skrebensky near the close of *The Rainbow:*

> Then there in the great flare of light, she clinched hold of him, hard, as if suddenly she had the strength of destruction, she fastened her arms round him and tightened him in her grip, whilst her mouth sought his in a hard, rending, ever-increasing kiss, till his body was powerless in her grip, his heart melted in fear from the fierce, beaked, harpy's kiss. The water washed again over their feet, but she took no notice. She seemed unaware, she seemed to be pressing in her beaked mouth till she had the heart of him. Then, at last, she drew away and looked at him—looked at him. He knew what she wanted. He took her by the hand and led her across the foreshore, back to the sandhills. She went silently. He felt as if the ordeal of proof was upon him, for life or death. He led her to a dark hollow.
>
> "No, here," she said, going out to the slope full under the moonshine. She lay motionless, with wide-open eyes looking at the moon. He came direct to her, without preliminaries. She held him pinned down at the chest, awful. The fight, the struggle for consummation was terrible. It lasted till it was agony to his soul, till he succumbed, till he gave way as if dead, lay with his face buried, partly in her hair, partly in the sand, motionless now for ever, hidden away in the dark, buried, only buried, he only wanted to be buried in the goodly darkness, only that, and no more.
>
> He seemed to swoon. It was a long time before he came to himself. He was unaware of an unusual motion of her breast. He looked up. Her face lay like an image in the moonlight, the eyes wide open, rigid. But out of her eyes, slowly, there rolled a tear, that glittered in the moonlight as it ran down her cheek.
>
> He felt as if the knife were being pushed into his already dead body. With head strained back, he watched, drawn tense, for some minutes, watched the unaltering, rigid face like metal in the moonlight, the fixed, unseeing eye, in which slowly the water gathered, shook with glittering moonlight, then surcharged, brimmed over and ran trickling, a tear with its burden of moonlight, into the darkness, to fall in the sand.

In his great poem, "Tortoise Shout," Lawrence epitomized the gnosis of Skrebensky's "bitterness of ecstasy":

> Why were we crucified into sex?
> Why were we not left rounded off, and finished in ourselves,
> As we began,
> As he certainly began, so perfectly alone?

Lawrence's unique power, as a prophetic novelist, tends now to make even his admirers a touch uneasy. In his later novels, such as *Kangaroo* (1923) and *The Plumed Serpent* (1926), as well as *Lady Chatterley's Lover* (1928), the literary artist is overcome by the prophet, and Lawrence bruises the limits of narrative, making it difficult to reread him with sustained attention. But in *The Rainbow* and *Women in Love* we trust the tales, and not their teller. ❦

Biography of D. H. Lawrence

Born David Herbert Richards Lawrence on September 11, 1885, the fourth son of Arthur Lawrence, a miner, and Lydia Beardsall Lawrence, D. H. Lawrence produced works in his 44 years of life that provoked controversy and scandal in his day and that have endured to ours for their acute insight into the regularly confrontational and often fragile relationships found in families and between the sexes.

Lawrence received more schooling than usual for a collier's son. During his school years, he began frequent visits to the Chambers family at their farm where his friendship with Jessie Chambers, the model for Miriam Leivers of *Sons and Lovers,* developed. He continued his schooling by winning scholarships and placing first in divisional exams so that by 1908 he qualified for a normal school teaching certificate. In the meantime, in late 1910, Lawrence broke his engagement to Jessie Chambers. She continued a friendship with Lawrence and read the first draft of *Sons and Lovers* in the autumn of 1911. After the break, Lawrence became engaged to Louie Burrows, a fellow teaching student and later headmistress of schools. While teaching, Lawrence published his first poems, with the help of Ford Madox Hueffer (Ford), and his first novel entitled *Laetitia,* later published as *The White Peacock* (1911). That same year, his teaching career was cut short due to a case of pneumonia.

During these years of early writing and changing relationships, Lawrence's work was often interrupted by poor health. In February of 1912, Lawrence ended the engagement with Louie Burrows citing his illness as the cause for the break. In March, Lawrence met Ernest Weekley and his German wife Frieda, a titled member of the aristocratic Von Richthofen family. Frieda believed in sexual liberation and although married had had several affairs before meeting Lawrence. They began a relationship almost immediately but kept it private. Shortly thereafter, around the time that Lawrence last saw Jessie Chambers, Lawrence revealed his relationship with Frieda in a letter to Edward Garnett of Duckworth Publishers. Even through the many difficult times ahead, from 1912 on Frieda was part of D. H. Lawrence's life.

His novel *The Trespasser* was published in 1912. In March of the following year, 1913, Lawrence and Frieda were served with divorce papers by Ernest Weekley. *Sons and Lovers* was published shortly thereafter by Duckworth which advanced Lawrence £100 for the novel. Frieda Weekley's divorce, in which she lost all contact with her three children, became final in April 1914. She and Lawrence married in July of that year. During this time period, Lawrence worked on drafts of *The Sisters,* versions that later evolved into *The Rainbow* and *Women in Love.*

In the war years from 1914 to 1918, the Lawrences lived for a time in Cornwall, England and maintained a close relationship with John Middleton Murry and Katherine Mansfield who were the witnesses at their wedding. The Lawrences were considered part of a fashionable literary set. At this time, Lawrence formed a friendship with Lady Ottoline Morrell, the supposed model for the character Hermione Roddice in *Women in Love.* D. H. Lawrence also met the philosopher Bertrand Russell and intellectuals from Cambridge. Despite attempts to convince them about his utopian society called 'Rananim', Lawrence quickly determined that they could not be revolutionary enough in their individual lives to accept his view of a life liberated from society. It is not surprising that Lawrence favored such a vision. The Lawrences were evicted from their Cornwall cottage on the suspicion of spying. Once in Berkshire, Lawrence worked on revisions to *Women in Love* while he published more poems and short stories.

Lawrence's health continued to decline in the years 1919 to 1920 when he and Frieda traveled to Florence, Sicily, and Sardinia. *Women in Love* was finally published in 1920, along with *The Lost Girl.* The next year, Lawrence finished writing *Aaron's Rod,* published later in 1922. Frieda and Lawrence, having made plans to visit America, began a long trip with that destination in mind, first stopping in Ceylon, then Australia, and finally arriving in California by way of the South Sea Islands. During this time, his novel *Kangaroo* was published in 1923. They settled in Taos, New Mexico at the invitation of Mabel Dodge Luhan who had organized a colony of artists at her ranch. Despite suffering his first pulmonary hemorrhage, Lawrence and Frieda managed a trip to Mexico at this time and then spent three years at Kiowa Ranch. Mabel Luhan offered to sell them the ranch; instead, they exchanged the manuscript of *Sons and Lovers* for the ranch.

In 1925, Lawrence finished *The Plumed Serpent* but fell gravely ill with typhoid and pneumonia. He was diagnosed with tuberculosis and recuperated at Kiowa Ranch. Around this time, Dorothy Brett, an aspiring painter, became Lawrence's disciple who often typed his manuscripts and traveled with the Lawrences. Lawrence and Frieda returned to Europe that year and settled in Spotorno, Italy. It was at this time that Frieda met Angelo Ravagli, her future lover and lifelong companion. Frieda frequently took trips to visit her family or made other pretences so that she could spend time with Ravagli such that in the following year, while Lawrence wrote *The Virgin and the Gypsy*, the relationship between Lawrence and Frieda suffered from serious quarrels. Lawrence attempted a brief affair with Dorothy Brett and then reconciled with Frieda. Lawrence returned to England for a last visit in the late summer of 1926. On his return to Italy, he began the first version of *Lady Chatterley's Lover*. His friendship with Aldous Huxley and his wife Maria was established at this time. In 1927, Lawrence finished the second version of *Lady Chatterley's Lover* and in the fall of that year made plans to publish the work privately with Pino Orioli to avoid the obstacles he had experienced when publishing earlier works. Nevertheless, when Lawrence had the third and final version of *Lady Chatterley's Lover* ready for publication in Florence in 1928, he encountered legal complications in delivering copies to private subscribers in Great Britain and the United States.

The following year, Lawrence traveled to Paris to arrange for a cheap edition of *Lady Chatterley's Lover*. He and Frieda also traveled to Majorca, France, and Bavaria. Lawrence spent most of the year writing poems and short texts and in the company of his friends, the Huxleys and Earl and Achsah Brewster. His health deteriorated such that Lawrence entered the Ad Astra Sanatorium in Vence in February, 1930. He discharged himself from the sanatorium on March 1, 1930 and died the next day at Villa Robermond in Vence. Five years later, Frieda sent Angelo Ravagli—they married in 1950—to Vence to have the body of D. H. Lawrence exhumed, cremated, and the ashes brought back to Kiowa Ranch in Taos, New Mexico where Frieda died in 1956. ❦

Plot Summary of
Sons and Lovers

(Citations are taken from Lawrence, D. H. *Sons and Lovers*. David Trotter, ed. Oxford: Oxford University Press, 1995.)

Begun as *Paul Morel*, the work was started and stopped several times until Lawrence finished the text in April of 1912. He revised a third version, and then finished revisions on the fourth and final version in November 1912, which Duckworth of London published in May 1913 entitled as it is today, *Sons and Lovers*.

Lawrence divides his story of Paul Morel and his family in two parts roughly corresponding to Paul's passage from adolescence into manhood. In the first chapter, entitled **The Early Married Life of the Morels,** Mrs. Morel takes some pride in occupying an end house in "The Bottoms", a poor mining neighborhood. As the story begins, she is expecting a third and unwanted child. She must manage in the poverty she finds next to her drunken husband. Lawrence describes their courtship and the early happiness which soon disappears when drunken brawls become frequent. She comes to despise Morel and puts all her hopes in her son William. Then in **The Birth of Paul, and Another Battle,** the baby she did not want turns into the center of her being. In another drunken and violent outburst, Mr. Morel throws a kitchen drawer at his wife while she holds the baby. It grazes her face and draws blood though she bends over to protect the baby. Though Morel helps dress the wound, the damage between the two is done. In **The Casting Off of Morel—The Taking on of William,** Morel falls ill. Morel's recuperation brings them close again and soon a fourth baby, Arthur, is born. As time passes, Mrs. Morel defends and protects her children no matter the circumstances. She joins the Women's Guild, a group attached to Co-operative Wholesale Society. At 13, William gets a job at the Co-op office. When he turns over his pay to her, she gives him an allowance which William uses to go dancing, much to her dismay. But William progresses and moves on to a job in Nottingham and later one in London for which he must leave home: "It never occurred to him that she might be more hurt at his going away than glad of his success. Indeed, as the days drew nearer for his departure, her heart began to close and grow dreary with despair."(66)

'The Young Life of Paul' reveals that the family has moved from The Bottoms to a house with a view of the valley; but the children hate it and their father. Paul prays nightly to make his father stop drinking. Slowly Morel is shut off from the family affairs. In rare pleasant moments, the children enjoy the fact that Morel can cobble and is a good storyteller, but they only feel secure when their father is asleep. Paul is a sickly child and often sleeps with mother. Gradually, in William's absence, Paul becomes his mother's companion. Friday nights are the only pleasant times, set aside for baking and Mrs. Morel's marketing. Paul, Annie, and Arthur play by the lamp-post until after dark on these happier evenings. Then William comes home for his first visit at Christmas causing great excitement; on his departure, though, sadness returns to the household.

Paul Launches into Life begins when Paul is fourteen. Mr. Morel is injured seriously at work and must be hospitalized. William's career continues to progress. Since Paul is out of school, his mother decides to help him find work and then accompanies him on the train to his interview at Jordan's Manufacturing. Though Paul is reluctant to take the job, his mother insists. Later, Mrs. Morel comments that William no longer sends money home. The reason is a girl named 'Gyp', his nickname for Louisa Western. In the meantime, Paul has his first day of work and when, on his return home, he gazes from the train at the lights of the town: "He felt rich in life and happy." (130) Nightly, like Scheherazade, Paul tells his mother stories of his day's activities. In **Death in the Family** the family seems to move on with life—Arthur is at school, Annie teaching, William engaged, and Paul is at home—but all still loathe Mr. Morel. William arrives with Gyp for a visit causing immediate tension in the family. At another point, when Paul has a holiday from work his mother proposes an outing. His very fond reply ("I say, little woman, how lovely!") (140) emphasizes the tender relationship that has grown between mother and son. They spend the day visiting the Leivers family at Willey Farm. After tea with Mrs. Leivers they "went out into the wood that was flooded with bluebells, while fumy forget-me-nots were in the paths. The mother and son were in ecstasy together." (145) This happy scene is followed by another difficult visit from William and Gyp. William criticizes his fiancée but he is determined to marry her because, as he tells his mother, their relationship has gone too far. Shortly after his return to London, he falls gravely ill. Mrs. Morel arrives in

London shortly before William dies. Paul is sixteen at this time and becomes seriously ill not long after the funeral.

The second part of the novel begins with **Lad-and-Girl Love** when Miriam Leivers, beautiful and almost 16, and Paul slowly wake up to love. Miriam, unlike most girls in her circumstances, has a desire to learn, resents her household chores, and is largely indifferent to boys. In the scenes at Willey Farm, Lawrence brings color into the text frequently. The young couple discover a common appreciation for nature and talk often of the flowers they see. As their friendship progresses, Paul shares books and his sketches with her. But Miriam, instead, seeks a communion with Paul, a holy connection demanding emotional commitment and avoiding all physical contact. Here Lawrence introduces Miriam's idea of love as sacrifice when she decides she will, if necessary, surrender her body to him. On a family holiday at the seashore, Miriam's purity prevents their first kiss.

In **Strife in Love** Arthur finishes his apprenticeship but remains wild and restless. He enlists in the Army and immediately regrets it. Mrs. Morel continues to take pride though in Paul. Tension persists between Paul and Miriam who introduces him to Clara Dawes, an older woman separated from her husband, Baxter. At this time, Paul begins to question religion and the zealous Miriam suffers from his doubts. Spring is the worst time for Paul as he now wants passion but resists it. They share French lessons on Friday nights. One night at home, Paul tells his mother he no longer wants Miriam in his life. Around this time, his mother shows signs of ill health. In **Defeat of Miriam** Paul remains dissatisfied with himself and everything. Miriam, at 20, feels the fullness of womanhood yet anticipates disaster. She uses daffodils one day to start a conversation when suddenly Paul announces they should split. Miriam blames the break on his family. Paul still visits Willey Farm and when Miriam invites both Paul and Clara to the farm, in an aside, Paul and Edgar Leivers wonder if Clara is a "man-hater". Later, when he speaks to his mother about Clara, Mrs. Morel tells him he needs a 'good woman'.

Annie's wedding then frames two events: Paul tells his mother he will never marry and Mrs. Morel decides to buy her son Arthur out of the army. Life changes around Paul as his siblings move on and the triangle of tension between Paul, Miriam, and Clara develops. Miriam is clearly bitter and tortured by Paul's interest in Clara. Then in a letter to Miriam, Paul ends their relationship. He is 23 and a virgin. In the chapter **Clara,** the family progresses, only Mr. Morel remains unchanged. Paul wins another prize for a landscape which he sells. Paul goes out socially and Arthur marries. Taking a message to Clara at her mother's home gives Paul the chance to see her in a different context. Clara returns to work at Jordan's but keeps apart from other workers. When the girls at work give Paul paints for his birthday, Clara feels left out and secretly leaves a book of poems for him. The gift causes Paul to approach her. On a walk, they talk of her marriage and Clara unexpectedly questions Paul why he avoids intimacy with Miriam if he loves her. As Lawrence reveals in **The Test on Miriam,** Paul is "bound in by their own virginity" (316) like other men of his day, but he starts seeing Miriam again. By this point Mrs. Morel has given up her battle against Miriam. At Willey Farm, Paul reveals his love to Miriam. Although she kisses him first, Miriam retains her idea of sex as being a sacrifice. Later Miriam stays at her grandmother's cottage alone, Paul visits and Miriam's sacrifice becomes a reality. But Paul returns home and tells mother he will not see Miriam anymore. Clara's presence draws him away and another break-up with Miriam occurs; this time Miriam attributes the split to Clara.

In the chapter **Passion,** Paul tells Clara of the separation, kisses her and is deliriously happy. On a riverside walk, they must go a long way to find privacy and become intimate at last. Paul is so madly in love he does not realize that Mrs. Morel's health worsens. Then mother and son talk of marriage and Clara. When Clara visits Paul at home, she meets his mother and father and experiences both enjoyment and fear. A resentful Miriam stops by and observes them together. Later, after going to theater, Paul spends the night at Clara's house where they are intimate while her mother sleeps.

The focus shifts when the chapter **Baxter Dawes** opens as Paul runs into Dawes in a pub where he tries to start a fight. When Paul recounts this later, he and Clara quarrel. An altercation between Dawes and Paul at work involves Mr. Jordan and results in Dawes losing his job. Paul's and Clara's relationship becomes public knowledge. Nevertheless, both start to drift apart and Clara begins to consider the differences between Paul and Dawes. One night while walking home in the dark Paul is attacked by Dawes and left unconscious. When he revives, his thoughts are only for his mother. At this time, the family discovers that Mrs. Morel, who is visiting at Annie's home, has an inoperable tumor. The children bring her home to die.

In **The Release** through his mother's doctor, Paul learns that Baxter Dawes is hospitalized with typhoid. He senses a connection with Dawes; first because of Clara and now due to the fight. Paul visits him in hospital where the two men use the neutral subject of the sick mother to break the tension. When Paul tells Clara, she becomes hostile and visits Dawes soon thereafter. His mother's illness strains Paul's relationship with Clara further. Annie and Paul tend to their mom and one evening increase her dose of morphine to help her sleep. She dies the next day. Paul sits with his dead mother and mourns his profound loss. Only when she sees Paul and Dawes together later, does Clara clearly compare the two men in her mind. She rejects Paul's half-heartedness and begs Dawes to take her back. In the final chapter, **Derelict,** all involved go their separate ways. Paul spends his time adrift and often drunk. He invites Miriam, on her way to an independent life as a teacher, to dinner in his new apartment. To Paul, she now looks older than Clara. Miriam mentions marriage but as an ultimatum: marriage or nothing. They part again and finally; Miriam embittered because her sacrifice has been refused. Now truly on his own, Paul cries out for his mother. Rejecting defeat, he chooses life. ❦

List of Characters in
Sons and Lovers

Walter Morel: A gruff and sometimes violent miner who causes more harm than good to his family, Mr. Morel drinks away his earnings and soon is despised by both his wife and his children. His positive points, being handy and a good storyteller, are overshadowed by his abusive nature and alcoholic outbursts.

Gertrude Coppard Morel: Outwardly a long-suffering wife, Gertrude Morel is a creative woman of vision and ambition. Early on in her marriage, she comes to despise her alcoholic husband and directs all her inner strength and skill to further her children's fortune in life. Mrs. Morel becomes much more than her son Paul's companion in life; she is his model for love and as such an obstacle to developing an independent sense of self and an idea of love for other women.

William Morel: The first son and the one for whom Mrs. Morel had most ambitious hopes, William is educated and quite successful by the family's standards. Then distracted and ultimately defeated by his attraction for Gyp, William focuses more on pleasing outward and passing needs than pursuing the potential allotted him by his education and employment. In a tragic twist of fate, William frees himself from social and family demands only by contracting a virulent skin infection.

Annie Morel: The second child, Annie avoids her father but enjoys taking care of and playing with Paul. She becomes a teacher in a local school and marries.

Paul Morel: The central character of the story is the third child and second son of the family. Paul is a sickly child who consequently spends a great deal of time with his mother. As Mrs. Morel distances herself more from her husband, Paul becomes his mother's companion. He does not perform as well as William in school but focuses his creative energy on painting. As Paul grows out of adolescence, his mother shifts between holding and losing his attention in favor of the love Paul seeks with Miriam and Clara.

Arthur Morel: The third boy in the Morel family is handsome but short-tempered like his father. He is not interested in further schooling and instead of work, Arthur enlists in the army only to regret his decision.

Clara Dawes: Outwardly independent, Clara has educated herself, supports the suffragette movement and leaves her husband to live on her own. She becomes Paul's lover during her estrangement from her husband, Baxter Dawes, another employee at Jordan Manufacturing. Ultimately, Clara returns to the clarity of the relationship with her husband in preference to the uncertainty surrounding Paul and his inability to define his feelings for Clara.

Miriam Leivers: Paul's almost constant companion of his early youth and his first love, Miriam never manages to get Paul to declare himself fully. When Miriam acquiesces to Paul's physical needs, she does so as a sacrifice to God. Not surprisingly, Mrs. Morel never approves of Miriam. Miriam introduces Paul to Clara Dawes and becomes embittered as a relationship develops between them.

The Leivers Family: Of the members in the family, Paul develops special bonds with Mrs. Leivers, Edgar, the oldest boy and Miriam. The Leivers live on a farm some distance away which Paul visits frequently. Their life on the farm is so different than that in the Morel household that Paul enjoys the change, the landscape, and the companionship offered by the family.

Baxter Dawes: A worker at Jordan's Manufacturing, Baxter is also Clara's estranged husband who leaves Paul Morel unconscious one night after a brutal fight. Later, Dawes and Morel forge an uneasy but significant alliance based on their enmity and their shared intimacy with Clara.

Louisa Lily Denys Western ("Gyp"): Miss Western becomes engaged to William and quickly earns the disdain of Mrs. Morel and Paul who see through Gyp's thin exterior. Orphaned and socially vulnerable, Gyp appeals to William for care and support. Despite her intellectual emptiness and irresponsibility, Gyp succeeds in winning William away from his ambitions to provide her with the security and possessions she demands. ❈

Critical Views on
Sons and Lovers

LETTER FROM D. H. LAWRENCE TO EDWARD GARNETT

[Lawrence describes the story of *Sons and Lovers* here to the editor from Duckworth Publishers. As he mentions in correspondence to others when announcing a new novel, Lawrence believes he has written 'a great book'. Later he and Garnett will have serious problems resulting from Garnett's editing of the *Sons and Lovers* manuscript.]

To Edward Garnett, from Villa Igéa, Gargnano, Italy, 14 November 1912

Dear Garnett: Your letter has just come. I hasten to tell you I sent the MS. of the *Paul Morel* novel to Duckworth registered, yesterday. And I want to defend it, quick. I wrote it again, pruning it and shaping it and filling it in. I tell you it has got form—*form*: haven't I made it patiently, out of sweat as well as blood. It follows this idea: a woman of character and refinement goes into the lower class, and has no satisfaction in her own life. She has had a passion for her husband, so the children are born of passion, and have heaps of vitality. But as her sons grow up she selects them as lovers—first the eldest, then the second. These sons are *urged* into life by their reciprocal love of their mother—urged on and on. But when they come to manhood, they can't love, because their mother is the strongest power in their lives, and holds them. It's rather like Goethe and his mother and Frau von Stein and Christiana—As soon as the young men come into contact with women, there's a split. William gives his sex to a fribble, and his mother holds his soul. But the split kills him, because he doesn't know where he is. The next son gets a woman who fights for his soul—fights his mother. The son loves the mother—all the sons hate and are jealous of the father. The battle goes on between the mother and the girl, with the son as object. The mother gradually proves stronger, because of the tie of blood. The son decides to leave his soul in his mother's hands, and, like his elder brother go for passion. He gets passion. Then the split begins to tell again. But, almost unconsciously, the mother realises what is the matter, and begins to die. The son casts off his mistress, attends to his mother dying. He is left in the end naked of everything, with the drift towards death.

It is a great tragedy, and I tell you I have written a great book. It's the tragedy of thousands of young men in England—it may even be Bunny's tragedy. I think it was Ruskin's, and men like him. —Now tell me if I haven't worked out my theme, like life, but always my theme. Read my novel. It's a great novel. If *you* can't see the development—which is slow, like growth—I can.

As for the *Fight for Barbara*—I don't know much about plays. If ever you have time, you might tell me where you find fault with the *Fight for Barbara. The Merry Go Round* and the other are candidly impromptus. I *know* they want doing again—recasting. I should like to have them again, now, before I really set to work on my next novel—which I have conceived—and I should like to try re-casting and re-forming them. If you have time, send them me.

I should like to dedicate the *Paul Morel* to you—may I? But not unless you think it's really a good work. 'To Edward Garnett, in Gratitude.' But you can put it better.

You are miserable about your play. Somehow or other your work riles folk. Why does it? But it makes them furious. Nevertheless, I shall see the day when a volume of your plays is in all the libraries. I can't understand why the dreary weeklies haven't read your *Jeanne* and installed it as a 'historical document of great value.' You know they hate you as a creator, all the critics: but why they shouldn't sigh with relief at finding you—in their own conceptions—a wonderfully subtle renderer and commentator of history, I don't know.

Pinker wrote me the other day, wanting to place me a novel with one of the leading publishers. Would he be any good for other stuff? It costs so many stamps, I don't reply to all these people.

Have I made those naked scenes in *Paul Morel* tame enough? You cut them if you like. Yet they are so clean—and I *have* patiently and laboriously constructed that novel.

It is a marvellous moonlight night. The mountains have shoulder-capes of snow. I have been far away into the hills today, and got great handfuls of wild Christmas roses. This is one of the most beautiful countries in the world. You must come. The sunshine is marvellous, on the dark blue water, the ruddy mountains' feet, and the snow.

F. and I keep struggling forward. It is not easy, but I won't complain. I suppose, if in the end I can't make enough money by writing, I shall have to go back to teaching. At any rate I can do that, so matters are never hopeless with me.

When you have time, do tell me about the *Fight for Barbara.* You think it couldn't be any use for the stage? I think the new generation is rather different from the old. I think they will read me more gratefully. But there, one can only go on.

It's funny, there is not *war* here—except 'Tripoli.' Everybody sings 'Tripoli'. The soldiers howl all the night through and bang tambourines when the wounded heroes come home. —And the Italian papers are full of Servia and Turkey—but what has England got to do with it?

It's awfully good of you to send me a paper. But you'll see, one day I can help you, or Bunny. And I will.

You sound so miserable. It's the damned work. I wish you were here for awhile. If you get run down, do come quickly. *Don't* let yourself become ill. This is such a beastly dangerous time. And you could work here, and live cheap as dirt with us.

Don't mind if I am impertinent. Living here alone one gets so different—sort of *ex cathedra.*

>   —D. H. Lawrence, "Letter to Edward Garnett." In *The Collected Letters of D. H. Lawrence*, Volume 1, ed. Henry T. Moore (New York: Viking, 1962): pp. 160–162.

Judith Arcana on Mother-Blaming in *Sons and Lovers*

> [Professor Arcana, author of *Grace Paley's Life Stories: A Literary Biography* (1993), states in this essay that she does not want to further the tendency in Lawrentian criticism to apply the Freudian Oedipal hypothesis to another analysis of *Sons and Lovers*. She ascribes as well the trend toward mother-blaming to the responsibilities attributed to a

mother—and never removed from her—by our culture. In this essay, Arcana claims that *Sons and Lovers* does not exhibit as much mother-blaming as the critics imply. Here, she gives some historical perspective on the reception of the book and the central mother figure, Mrs. Morel.]

Sons and Lovers does not contain the wholesale mother-blaming so many scholars claim to find in it. The character of Gertrude Morel, like the delineation of her relations with her husband and children, is far too complex to be accommodated within such a reductive analysis. Notwithstanding that complexity—and the rich field it offers for scholarly pursuit—most contemporary critics have attempted to make up for Lawrence's omission by assuming or even insisting, often with anger and hostility, that mother-blaming is present in the novel—as theme, characterization, subtext, or narrative form.

Lawrence's contemporaries received the book—and Mrs. Morel—in a different mood. They, like Ralph Waldo Emerson, may well have held mothers responsible for the behavior of their sons; certainly, in the England of 1913, they were by no means free of misogyny. But few had studied—or even heard of—Freud's theories. Reviewers of the newly published novel found Mrs. Morel "heroic," Paul "super-human[ly] selfish," and the theme of the book to be simply the normal "struggle . . . between his devotion to his mother and the clamorous passion of his early manhood." Mrs. Morel's raising of her son was respected as a mother's "life-long effort"; she is considered "a good housewife and decent woman." "The mother is a creature of superb and lovable heroism," said one critic, admitting that "she is sometimes downright disagreeable." Gertrude is "noble," "splendid," "strong of will, rich in love and sympathy, a fine, true woman, into the very core." In fact, most critics in 1913 were not disturbed to find that the "love for each other of the mother and her son . . . is the mainspring of both their lives . . . portrayed tenderly, yet with a truthfulness which [reveals] that friction which is unavoidable between the members of two different generations." Thus spake those to whom Sigmund Freud was—if anyone at all—merely a Viennese doctor of dubious reputation, and to whom Oedipus was simply an ill-fated mythical king. Philip Wylie, whose coining of the term "momism" marked the beginning of the open libel and slander of mothers at mid-century, was yet an unforeseen complication of family life.

In 1932, it was still possible for Aldous Huxley to resist the Freudian tide in biographical criticism and assert that Lawrence would have been "essentially and fundamentally" the same "even if his mother had died when he was a child." But by the mid-sixties, Alfred Kazin had written of Freud as "the *discoverer* of the Oedipus complex," and Daniel Weiss had declared that Lawrence's work "is colored by the psychological *discoveries* of the twentieth century" [my emphasis], both implying thus that the constellation of roles and traits Freud had invented, to explain a phenomenon he posited through his practice, was organic, biologically or psychologically present in humankind—and forcefully manifested in the fiction of D.H. Lawrence.

Subsequently, especially in recent years, literary critics have often employed Freud's theories and terms—or variations of them—in their mother-blaming assault upon Gertrude Morel. This is wholly in keeping with the growth of mother-blaming in the culture-at-large, though ironically at odds with the common critical perspective on modern poets and writers of fiction. ⟨...⟩

> —Judith Arcana, "I Remember Mama: Mother-Blaming in *Sons and Lovers* Criticism," *The D.H. Lawrence Review* 21, no. 2 (Delaware: University of Delaware, Summer 1989): pp. 139–140.

HELEN BARON ON LAWRENCE'S *SONS AND LOVERS* VERSUS GARNETT'S

> [Helen Baron edited the 1992 Cambridge edition of *Sons and Lovers*. This essay traces differences in the edition as a result of the emendations made by Edward Garnett of Duckworth Publishers with the modern edition. In this excerpt, Professor Baron refers to the library episode in Chapter VII and explains the disparities found in the two texts in Paul and Miriam's interactions.]

⟨...⟩ Lawrence portrayed Paul as interested in the wider impact of evolutionary theory on sociology and ethics. By the end of the conversation between Paul and Miriam as they leave the library, it becomes clear that Paul has been trying to rationalise the early death of his older brother William in terms of the survival of the spiritually fittest. He begins by rejecting the New Testament text which asserts the importance of the individual in Christian theology, 'Are not two sparrows sold for a farthing? and one of them shall not fall on the ground without your Father [knowing]. But the very hairs of your head are all numbered' (Matthew x. 29–30). His remarks, lifted out of the dialogue and strung together, are:

> It seems as if it didn't matter, one more or less, among the lot . . . I used to believe that about a sparrow falling—and hairs of the head—. . . Now I think that the race of sparrows matters, but not one sparrow: all my hair, but not one hair . . . And people matter. But *one* isn't so very important. Look at William . . . I call it only wasted . . . Waste and no more . . . Yet, I reckon we've got a proper way to go—and if we go it, we're all right—and if we go near it. But if we go wrong, we die. I'm sure our William went wrong somewhere . . . What we are inside makes us so that we ought to go one particular way and no other.

Garnett may have had no better reason for cutting the whole 135-line episode than that it was a convenient section to remove in order to shorten the novel, but the novel is significantly impoverished without it, and in removing it Garnett cut a dialogue that reflected on one of the burning intellectual issues of the day.

Here again, Herbert Spencer is in the wings. The stark ideological choice implied by this issue is indicated in the section dealing with Spencer under the entry on Sociology in the *Encyclopaedia Britannica* of 1910: 'in the evolution of society, natural selection will in its characteristic result reach the individual not directly, but through society. That is to say, in social evolution, the interests of the individual *qua* individual, cease to be a matter of first importance'. On the one hand 'Spencer has been for long accepted by the general mind as the modern writer who more than any other has brought into use the term "social organism," and who has applied the doctrine of evolution to the theory of its life'. On the other hand the writer of this entry in the *Encyclopaedia* took the logical conclusion to be that the individual is therefore subordinate to the *state* and he described Spencer's *Principles of Sociology* as 'futile' because Spencer preferred a 'conception of social organism "in which the corporate life must be subservient to the lives of the parts"'.

In the light of this debate, Paul's reference to sparrows serves several purposes. It is an additional detail in the novel's characterisation of him as enjoying theological discussion. It indicates that he is preoccupied with the challenge posed by the evolution debate to New Testament theology. But, in addition, his extrapolation of the New Testament text in terms of 'the *race* of sparrows' suggests that he sees the question of the individual versus the group in biological and racial rather than political and national terms. This helps to explain why the word 'natural' takes on such significance in the novel.

—Helen Baron, "Lawrence's *Sons and Lovers* versus Garnett's," *Essays in Criticism* 42, no. 4 (Oxford: Summer 1992): pp. 270–271.

Helen Baron on Disseminated Consciousness

[Helen Baron edited the 1992 Cambridge edition of *Sons and Lovers*. This essay traces differences in the edition as a result of the emendations made by Edward Garnett of Duckworth Publishers with the modern edition. In this excerpt, Professor Baron further explains the disparities found in the two texts.]

One of the large understated questions in *Sons and Lovers* is the extent to which individuals are not in control of their own destiny, circumstances, and even their moment-to-moment experiences. Lawrence formulates the idea early in the opening chapter: 'Sometimes life takes hold of one, carries the body along, accomplishes one's history, and yet is not real, but leaves one's self as it were slurred over.' Such rare authorial philosophising is like a vestigial trace of George Eliot's influence. Thereafter in *Sons and Lovers* the topic is explored through the narrator's reportage: the characters' thoughts, their experiences of the 'self', Paul's reflections on 'fate' and so on, as when Paul comments to Miriam: 'But you are what your unconscious self makes you, not so much what you want to be.' In addition, the boundary between 'life' and 'self' is constantly questioned by the narrator's unusual use of vocabulary and syntax. Grammar that seems misaligned dissolves the barriers separating individuals from each other or their surroundings and probes the problematic relationship between identity and consciousness.

In the complete text of the novel the words 'conscious', 'unconscious' and 'self-conscious', occur so often that the reader is led to ponder the ways in which the novel addresses issues of 'psychology' and challenges our very use of the word 'consciousness'. The four occurrences in the first chapter all arise in the aftermath of the Morels' quarrel, when Walter locks Gertrude out of the house and 'she could not control her consciousness'. In the powerfully-written and much-quoted climax to that episode Lawrence presents Mrs Morel as vividly experiencing a loss of 'self':

> Mrs Morel leaned on the garden gate, looking out, and she lost herself awhile. She did not know what she thought. Except for a slight feeling of sickness, and her consciousness in the child, her self melted out like scent into the shiny, pale air. After a time, the child too melted with her in the mixing-pot of moonlight, and she rested with the hills and lilies and houses, all swum together in a kind of swoon.

This is more than an elaborate description of 'a kind of swoon': it raises issues of identity and consciousness that will be taken up later in terms of the 'child' Paul's experience. Mrs Morel's single unitary identity is far less disrupted by the vocabulary of melting and swooning than by two quirks of grammar: *Except for* and *consciousness in*. Mrs Morel's 'self' melts *except for* her 'feeling' of sickness and her 'consciousness'. She is not conscious *of* the child, but her consciousness is located *in* the child. The narrator's unusual syntax has reinforced the impression that within Mrs Morel's totality her 'self', her 'feelings' and her 'consciousness' are separate parts which live in an undefined relationship to each other. 〈...〉

As the novel develops, its exploration of the relationship between states of consciousness and the nature of life at the level of cell structure becomes focussed on Paul as an artist. On the one hand he frequently experiences sensations of dissolving which parallel his mother's 'swoon' when pregnant with him; on the other hand his greater awareness of these sensations means that he can integrate them with his perceptions and theories about art. Soon after the session on the swing, Paul explains to Miriam the nature of his interest, as a painter, in plant biology: 'It's as if I'd painted the shimmering protoplasm in the leaves and everywhere, and not the stiffness of the shape'. When they are older and he has moved on from impressionist representations of plants to symmetrical William Morris-style roses, he justifies his new designs by reference to the effect of gravity on the cell-structure of plants, explaining to Miriam 'the theory that the force of gravitation is the great shaper, and that if it had all its own way, it would have a rose in correct geometrical line and proportion—and so on'.

In Chapter VIII, Paul's extended attempt to explain his theories of art to Miriam as they sit by lake 'Nethermere', re-invokes the word 'protoplasm' and re-produces in Paul a kind of waking nightmare version of the experience of cellular dissolution during his illness:

> He was discussing Michael Angelo. It felt to her as if she were fingering the very quivering tissue, the very protoplasm of life, as she heard him . . . There he lay in the white intensity of his search, and his voice gradually filled her with fear, so level it was, almost inhuman as if in a trance.
>
> 'Don't talk any more,' she pleaded softly, laying her hand on his forehead. He lay quite still, almost unable to move. His body was somewhere discarded . . .
>
> '. . . Even now, I look at my hands, and wonder what they are doing there. That water there ripples right through me. I'm sure I am that rippling. It runs right through me, and I through it. There are no barriers between us.'
> 'But—!' she stumbled.
> 'A sort of disseminated consciousness, that's all there is of me. I feel as if my body were lying empty, as if I were in the other things—clouds and water—'

Versions of this state of 'disseminated consciousness' recur in the novel, and they seem to indicate how it is that as an artist Paul is able to perceive things like the protoplasm beneath the surface of the leaves, and indeed to develop a sort of tactile imagination: 'The firmness and softness of her upright body could almost be felt as he looked at her'. His vision of Clara suggests the extraordinary plasticity of a sculptor's sensations while forming a clay model: 'In the glow, he could almost feel her as if she were present, her arms, her shoulders, her bosom, feel them, almost contain them'. What is outside him is experienced internally, almost as if he himself has a womb: 'he knew the curves of her breast and shoulders as if they had been moulded inside him.' In the presentation of Paul's unusual capacity for perceptions and sensations, Lawrence seems constantly to take his bearings from the ante-natal experience he had invented for Paul of sharing in his mother's swoon, when 'her self melted out like scent' and 'the child too melted with her in the mixing-pot of moonlight'. After all, from the perspective of a foetus in the womb, the connections between the 'self' and other entities are fluid, constantly forming and transforming. The portrayal of Paul Morel as an artist suggests that he has unusually free access to the pre-individuated state of consciousness, the 'unconscious'.

>—Helen Baron, "Disseminated Consciousness in *Sons and Lovers*," *Essays in Criticism* 48, no. 4 (Oxford: Oxford University Press, October 1998): pp. 357–358, 365–367.

Gerald Doherty on the Dialectic of Space

> [Gerald Doherty is the author of *Theorizing Lawrence: Nine Meditations on Tropological Themes* (1999). Professor Doherty maintains that the tension that Lawrence recreates between literal and figurative language is specially significant in this text, since spatial metaphors—open and closed spaces and boundaries—foment a liberation of meanings. The women in his life, Miriam, Clara, and his mother, represent spaces for Paul which he must manage in order to define and preserve his own in their absence.]

⟨. . .⟩ Miriam and Clara occupy the alternative poles of the dialectic between which Paul oscillates. But is there a middle ground between these extremes, one occupied by a character? In effect, Mrs. Morel inhabits this site, a space of comparative rest and consolidation, from which the oscillation between poles is judged and assessed. She occupies a kind of literal space, resistant to those radical metamorphoses of meaning to which all other spaces are subject: "There was one place in the world that stood solid and did not melt into unreality: the place where his mother was. Everyone else could grow shadowy, almost nonexistent to him (Paul), but she could not." Not herself subject to vacillation, she represents the base in the real upon which Paul imagines himself constructing a stable identity—"mak[ing] a man whom nothing should shift off his feet."

In dissolving this foundational space, Mrs. Morel's death creates a vacuum that voids the literal basis of sense, and that throws sense-making itself into question. It opens up a domain of non-meaning which no rhetoric can grasp or encompass. In representational terms, Mrs. Morel's death is opposed to her dying. Since the latter is an event *in time,* it possesses its own coherent narrative structure. It has a beginning (the first signs of the cancer), a developing middle (the cancer's slow depredations), and a dramatic denouement (the act of dying itself). Her death, by contrast, annuls precisely those temporal sequences that articulate narrative form; it assumes the dimensions of an uncircumscribed space ("There was no Time, only Space") without limits or closure. As such it is an event for which no narrative account exists. Because no narrative form can embrace it, it brings the narrative itself to an end.

The disclosure of this space commences with a typical distancing movement, a sharp swing of the dialectic away from the immediate context. In this instance, the movement is made via the tram-car that takes Paul away from his last tryst with Miriam: "(b)eyond the town the country, little smouldering spots for more towns—the sea—the night—on and on!" The night-space which, earlier internalized, transformed Paul into an "insecure, an indefinite thing" is now externalized. Self-generated, produced from within, it breathes forth again as a space without limits, at once here and nowhere, one that undoes the distinction between inner and outer: "From his breast, from his mouth, sprang the endless space, and it was there behind him, everywhere . . . (e)verywhere the vastness and terror of the immense night . . . holding everything in its silence and its living gloom."

In collapsing differences, this space also undoes the dialectic, dissolving the tension between open and closed. Paul seeks an object (his mother) who no longer exists, or who exists only in recession through the abysmal space that unmakes her: "Who could say his mother had lived and did not live . . . (n)ight, in which everything was lost, went reaching out, beyond stars and sun . . . (a)nd she was gone, intermingled herself." In effect, this spaceless space eradicates all distinctions, including the literal/metaphorical one that seemed to produce it. *Both* terms are marked by a lack: the literal by the blurring of well-defined referents, the absence of a proper orientation in space ("Where was he?—one tiny upright speck of flesh, less than an ear of wheat lost in the field. He could not bear it"); the metaphoric by an absence of images which seem to blur as they come into focus: "Stars and sun, a few bright grains, went spinning round for terror, and holding each other in embrace, there in a darkness that outpassed them all. . . ." In this dance of death, darkness is the all-enveloping milieu that obscures its own ghostly configurations at the same moment that it seems to evoke them.

—Gerald Dougherty, "The Dialectic of Space in D. H. Lawrence's *Sons and Lovers,*" *Modern Fiction Studies* 39, no. 2 (Purdue Research Foundation, Summer 1993): pp. 339–341.

Adrienne E. Gavin on the Labeling of Miriam Leivers

[Besides writing about Lawrence, Adrienne Gavin has published essays on Anna Sewell as well as on the Victorian novel. This essay—in the face of criticism both by characters in the text and literary critics—is a defense of Miriam Leivers since Gavin believes that the character has been mislabeled and reduced to images of her formed by others. In this excerpt, the focus is the small mirror in Miriam's room which permits Miriam to perceive an image of herself.]

⟨. . .⟩ Following Lawrence's famous advice to "never trust the teller, trust the tale," I believe a clue can be found in a small object nailed to Miriam's wall.

In her room is a mirror: "in the little looking glass nailed against the white-washed wall, she could only see a fragment of herself at a time." As she grows to womanhood she learns more about herself, sees herself more fully, and these fragments become a whole. She is similarly shown to the reader glance-by-glance. It is from aspects of character, incidents of behavior, and sentences of speech that we piece her together. Louis Martz describes the effect thus: "The image of Miriam appears and then is clouded over; it is as though we were looking at her through a clouded window that is constantly being cleared, and fogged, and cleared again."

Critics (and characters) are too often apt to take fragments as representative of the whole of Miriam's character, and the intertwining of the narrator's and Paul's points of view (which critics such as Martz and Daniel Schwarz discuss) has exacerbated this tendency and aided misreadings. "The girl was romantic in her soul" is, for example, often taken alone (as if against a "whitewashed wall") as the sum of her character, rather than as an introductory narratorial observation on a fifteen-year-old. Miriam's mirror is not only symbolic of her growth to maturity, and the fragmentary way in which she is revealed to the reader, but is also itself a part of her. Miriam serves as a mirror for other characters, particularly for Paul. Characters see reflected in Miriam something (generally negative) of themselves and consider this reflection representative of her total character.

In fact, she is often described in the novel as being in a shadow, or having her face shadowed: "[s]he stood beside him, for ever in shadow"; "[h]er face as she sat opposite was always in shadow." Whatever is in her shadows cannot "reflect," and so is often ignored. Her pain, her reasons for quietness, her intelligence, her hopes, her warmth, her love, and her natural, if hesitant, lust are often obscured. Paul does not see Miriam clearly, and is obsessed with what she reflects of himself. In an exchange with Clara Dawes, he ventures: "When she [woman] fights for herself she seems like a dog before a looking glass, gone into a mad fury with its own shadow." This image is reminiscent of the furies Paul gets into when he is confronted with Miriam's burgeoning physicality; he becomes angry at what she reflects, both physically and spiritually, of himself. Clara asks if *he* is the looking glass, and he replies, "Or the shadow," interestingly confusing "shadow" with "reflection." In a sense he puts Miriam in the shadows, then sees only what she reflects back of himself.

We see Miriam mainly in terms of her relationship with Paul, and that she falls deeply in love with him is often neglected as an influence on much of her "behavior." Paul is the more vocal of the two, and feels free to analyze Miriam. Some critics, indeed, judge her purely by his comments upon her, but Paul's "labels" do not in the end either adhere to Miriam or totally obscure her. He says to her of Clara "perhaps you like her because she's got a grudge against men," and the narrator comments, "That was more probably one of his own reasons for liking Mrs Dawes, but this did not occur to him." When narratorial comment is left out and Miriam is left silent, it may appear that she affirms Paul's comments about her. Her silence does not, however, usually signify assent; Diane Bonds, who points up Lawrence's labelling of Jessie Chambers, has demonstrated that a pattern exists: "Paul makes an assertion about Miriam; if she replies, she denies the assertion; Paul then reaffirms his initial statement; even if Miriam has previously attempted to argue, she may now 'shut up tight'—be quieted by chagrin, confusion, or frustration; if she should attempt to argue again, Paul changes the subject." Bonds also shows that Paul needs Miriam "to remain non-sexual and virginal"; he puts words between himself and her. While I would not agree that "Paul's speeches . . . beget Miriam's vision of her world and, to a certain extent, of herself," Bonds's argument does put things in proper perspective. Peter Balbert fundamentally misreads the text when he suggests that Paul's "sexual frustration becomes a reflection of his inability to pierce Miriam's self-protective shield of language." Miriam's (less effective) shield is silence; it is Paul in his eclecticism of emotion who uses language as a shield (and sword) against what Miriam reflects of himself and against seeing the rest of her clearly. Repeatedly we are told that he suddenly "hates" Miriam, that he gets into "such a tumult and fury. It ma[kes] her wretched."

—Adrienne E. Gavin, "Miriam's Mirror: Reflections on the Labelling of Miriam Leivers," *D. H. Lawrence Review* 21, no. 1 (Delaware: University of Delaware, Spring 1992): pp. 28–29.

ROBERT KIELY ON THE LANGUAGE AND POWER OF THE WORKING CLASS IN LAWRENCE'S FICTION

[The Loker Professor of English at Harvard University, Professor Kiely is the author of many books including *Beyond*

Egotism: The Fiction of James Joyce, Virginia Woolf, and D. H. Lawrence (1980) and *Reverse Tradition: Postmodern Fictions and the Nineteenth Century Novel* (1993). In this article, Professor Kiely focuses on the language of the mining communities as presented by Lawrence. This excerpt cites a passage where Mr. Morel speaks in his heavy dialect to provide an example of language as the exchange of useful information rather than a challenge to the family dynamic.]

The idea of language as a smoothly functioning tool for the exchange of practical and useful information is disrupted in a rich variety of ways in Lawrence's fiction, but where the working class is concerned the device readiest at hand is dialect. Most colliers in Lawrence's world turn dialect on and off at will; they play it like a musical instrument. It is a means of communication tuned to the mood of the moment rather than to the needs of an unreachable future. Its sounds, images, and rhythms establish harmonics that often thwart and mock the speech forms of those who are anxious about unambiguous meaning.

In the dialectics of the Morel family in *Sons and Lovers,* it is the mother in both her feminine and her bourgeois roles who, as a speaker of standard English, interprets and verifies the children's narrated experience: "No one told [the father] anything. The children, alone with their mother, told her all about the day's happenings, everything. Nothing had really taken place in them until it was told to their mother." Mrs. Morel validates and completes their half-finished sentences and adventures in her own heart. As a member of the bourgeoisie, she also, when the children grow older, translates their experiences into ambitions for education, a higher status, a better life.

Despite fits of drunkenness and rage, Mr. Morel rarely interferes with this closed family and linguistic circle. Occasionally, when things need fixing, Morel, "the good workman," sets happily about his task, singing and gathering his children around him for stories:

> "Tell us about down pit, daddy."
> This Morel loved to do.
> "Well, there's one little 'oss—we call 'im Taffy," he would begin. "An' he's a fawce 'un!"
> Morel had a warm way of telling a story. He made one feel Taffy's cunning.

"He's a brown 'un," he would answer, "an' not very high. Well, he comes i' th' stall wi' a rattle, an' then yo' 'ear 'im sneeze."

"''Ello, Taff,' you say, 'what art sneezin' for? Bin ta'ein' some snuff?'"

Such stories, we are told, could go on "interminably." They have no conclusion and no point. They do not invite interpretation or translation. Mrs. Morel never seems present during their telling and Mr. Morel's terms of affection—"my beauty," "my darlin'"—are directed at his children. Morel's stories in dialect are not presented as direct challenges to his wife's authority over him or their children. They are part of a verbal and emotional world apart, a language of non-cooperation, a whimsical refusal to join the discourse of practical sense. It is affective and playful language, not in the service of work (as defined by industry) yet unmistakably the language of the "good worker" since the text tells us that "these happy evenings could not take place unless Morel had some job to do." What is dislocated, then, is not Morel's identity as a laborer, but his function in an industrial mechanism and class structure that dominate his marriage and his life.

—Robert Kiely, "Out on Strike: The Language and Power of the Working Class in Lawrence's Fiction." In *The Challenge of D. H. Lawrence,* ed. Michael Squires and Keith Cushman (Madison: University of Wisconsin Press, 1990): pp. 94–95.

Margaret Storch on Images of Women in Lawrence

[Professor Storch has published several articles on Lawrence and Blake and has written on Frost's poetry. She bases the present critical work on the similarities between Blake and Lawrence "in their creative spirit and their ideals for individual life" (xi). Her approach when studying the affinities of both authors is psychoanalytical, founded on the work of

Melanie Klein more than Sigmund Freud. In this excerpt, Storch considers the episode where Paul sacrifices his sister Annie's doll.]

Beneath the more apparent triadic oedipal structure lie the dynamics of the early mother-infant dyad. The novel appears to be written out of loyalty to the mother, Gertrude Morel, on the part of the son, Paul Morel, whether against the aggressive father or the possessive sensual woman of the son's own generation; yet its true emotional core is a sense of hatred for the suffocating mother, leading to a series of fantasies in which the son destroys her, and culminating in her actual death at his hands. These key events are: the sacrifice of Annie's doll, Arabella, in Paul's childhood; the burning and symbolic entombment of the loaves of bread in the "Strife in Love" chapter; and the death of Gertrude Morel as an immediate result of an overdose of morphia administered by Paul. In each of them, we find a destructive anger that runs against the manifest devoted love for the mother in the text, corresponding to Melanie Klein's notion of the infantile defense mechanism of the splitting of the mother into a good aspect and a bad aspect.

The first episode is one of apparently motiveless violence in which the boy, Paul Morel, destroys his sister Annie's doll, with her frightened connivance:

> "Let's make a sacrifice of Arabella," he said. "Let's burn her."
> She was horrified, yet rather fascinated. She wanted to see what the boy would do. He made an altar of bricks, pulled some of the shavings out of Arabella's body, put the waxen fragments into the hollow face, poured on a little paraffin, and set the whole thing alight. He watched with wicked satisfaction the drops of wax melt off the broken forehead of Arabella, and drop like sweat into the flame. So long as the stupid big doll burned he rejoiced in silence. At the end he poked among the embers with a stick, fished out the arms and legs, all blackened, and smashed them under stones.
> "That's the sacrifice of Missis Arabella," he said. "An' I'm glad there's nothing left of her."

The scene cuts beneath the familiarly "oedipal" patterning of the novel to show a powerful anger against the mother. The "sacrifice" is an act of desecration against a figure who should be revered. This is apparent in the building of an altar, the title "Missis Arabella," and the aura of "wicked satisfaction" that emanates from defying a taboo. The body of the mother is, in fantasy, dismembered and destroyed, disintegrating in a flash of fiery consuming anger, and liquified into the wax and sweat of elemental fluids. When already blackened and "dead," the fragments are retrieved with aggressive phallic curiosity by means of a poking stick, and then further pulverized into nothingness, not "with" stones but "under" stones, suggesting both a final horror that cannot be looked at and the gravestones that cover the dead, which in turn have in their origins an impetus of aggression against the dead.

The scene is a vivid depiction of a child's sadistic fantasy against the mother. The presence of Annie is an essential component of the scene. In this and the cognate episodes, her witnessing of the event and her connivance at Paul's action suggest that part of the emotional totality of anger against the mother is a fantasy of a sibling relationship that is transmuted into relationships with female peers in defiance of the mother's sensuous dominance. The sister in earlier life can be a female figure who provides an alternative to the mother and who, like the son, strains against the mother's moral strictures.

—Margaret Storch, "Images of Women in Lawrence." In *Sons and Adversaries: Women in William Blake and D. H. Lawrence* (Knoxville: University of Tennessee Press, 1990): pp. 98–100.

Plot Summary of
The Rainbow

(Citations are from Lawrence, D. H. *The Rainbow*. Mark Kinkead-Weekes, ed. London: Penguin, 1995.)

Some parts of this text began during the years 1913–1914 as one of several drafts for *Women in Love*. Lawrence started the final version of the work, with the title of *The Rainbow,* in late 1914 with revisions taking him until May of 1915. Methuen of London published the novel that same year.

The Rainbow is the story of three generations of Brangwens, a family that for many years has owned and worked Marsh Farm in Nottinghamshire. In the opening chapter, **How Tom Brangwen Married a Polish Lady,** young Tom is not as good at school as his brothers. Rather, he does better on the farm and takes pride in assuming full management for it at the age of eighteen. After the death of his mother and father, Tom finds himself accompanied only by an old housekeeper. He is unlike his brothers too in his ability to stand alone and take responsibility. But, when at 19, he succumbs to lust and visits a prostitute, Tom suffers from a guilty conscience. Later a Polish widow, Lydia Lensky becomes the housekeeper for the vicar of the local church. She has a daughter, Anna, from her previous marriage, and despite better economic and social status earlier in life, Lydia appears determined to make a way for herself and her child. It takes Tom months to muster the courage to bring her daffodils one evening. They meet in the kitchen of the vicar's home and Tom manages to ask her to become his wife.

In the next chapter, **They Live at the Marsh,** judging by the standards of the day, their marriage is a successful one. Tom and Lydia later have two sons together, Tom Jr. and Fred. But Tom's favorite is his stepdaughter Anna. For him, it becomes easier to develop a relationship with the girl instead of her mother who always remained—perhaps because of a difference in language and culture—somewhat removed from her husband. Both experience times of reflection in their marriage when they recognize a lack of fulfillment in themselves and an emptiness in their union. On one occasion, Lydia even suggests that Tom take a lover. It is clear also in **Childhood of Anna Lensky** that young Anna is a conceited little girl who often imagines herself as a great lady or queen. She takes pleasure in accompanying Tom on his trips to market and speaking to the other men as if she were an adult. In the chapter **Girlhood of Anna Brangwen,** Anna is sent to the "dame's school" in town. She is shy and wild away from her father. By the time she attends Nottingham High School for Girls, Anna is a tall and awkward young girl. She grows to be restless and questioning and passes a time period espousing religious fervor. When she is eighteen, a nephew of Tom's, Will Brangwen, starts work at the lace factory in the nearby village. Will is only twenty years old. He stays at Marsh Farm where the Brangwens take care of him and make him part of their family. Though Anna shuns any intimacy at first, Anna and Will fall in love and show great and tender affection for each other. They surprise Tom and Lydia when they announce their plans to marry. Since Tom enjoys certain economic success from the farm, before the wedding he leases a home for the couple in the village which he furnishes with the latest appliances and give them a good deal of money to compensate for Will's low paying job.

Wedding at the March relates their wedding which is held with great ceremony and in which all in the area join in its merriment. Lawrence shifts from the mature and responsible Tom and Lydia to the young couple to show how Anna's willful character and William's passiveness do not mesh easily over the years. As described in the chapter **Anna Victrix,** the newlyweds spent the following two weeks shut away in their cottage enjoying the pleasures of married life so much that they barely leave the bedroom even for meals: "As they lay close together, complete and beyond the touch of time or change, it was as if they were at the very centre of all the slow wheeling of space . . ." (135) Anna is first to stir from their idyllic honeymoon. Later when she decides to give a tea party, this both bewilders and infuriates her husband who remains caught up in their initial passionate isolation. Will, then and throughout much of his marriage, finds it difficult to realize that they can not live wholly unto themselves. Nor does Will understand Anna's need to dance naked in her bedroom: "He watched, and his soul burned in him. He turned aside, he could not look, it hurt his eyes . . . It hurt him as he watched as if he were at the stake . . . The strangeness, the power in her dancing consumed him . . ." (171) They quarrel regularly and fiercely as they try to comprehend the increasing stress in their marriage caused by her demands and his normally compliant attitude. Anna feels smothered by Will but when she quickly becomes pregnant, her wishes for a son calm her. Lawrence calls attention to their struggles with words such as acquiescence, submission, and consummation.

In the chapter **The Cathedral** Anna and Will visit her mother's friend, the Baron Skrebensky. The Baron, who never really approved of Anna because she spoke no Polish, invites them to meet his wife and their young son Anton. The highlight of the trip for Will, though, involves a visit to Lincoln Cathedral which he considers "the perfect womb". (186) Anna is moved as well by the inner space but anger takes over her such that when she gets ". . . free from the cathedral, she had even destroyed the passion he had." (190) When Will realizes that Anna prefers to be a mother more than a married lover to him, he once again finds himself faced with a bewildering relationship. With each new year comes a new baby. Anna refuses to have much to do with her husband when she is not pregnant and seems to be happy only when she is expecting a child.

The first child is a girl, Ursula, who becomes her father's favorite. In the chapter **The Child,** as time passes, the love that Will would have preferred to give to his wife is directed instead to Ursula. In their second year married, Will rebels. At the theater one evening, he meets a girl whom he invites to dinner and a walk afterwards. This chaste but telling excursion provokes a change in the intimate life of Will and Anna. Passion increases between them enough so that during the day Will finds renewed calm, but at night he dominates his wife entirely, freeing himself eventually from her control. Around this time, Will returns his creative energy to carving, a hobby that occupies much of his spare time. The next chapter, **The Marsh and the Flood,** relates changes in the Brangwen family back on the Marsh. After Anna's marriage, her brothers Tom and Fred became the center of activity at the farm. The elder Tom Brangwen becomes a gentleman-farmer and with his wife Lydia lives a fairly comfortable life. Anna's intimacy with her father remains underdeveloped after her marriage and she prefers her mother's company more. Then suddenly Tom Brangwen dies one night as the result of an accident during a rain storm. On her own, Lydia begins to spend more time—until her own death—with her grandchildren with whom she enjoyed telling stories of coming to England and of her two husbands.

As the oldest, Ursula is responsible for taking her three sisters—Gudrun, Theresa, and Catherine—and young Billy to school. As she grows, Ursula always seeks out more. She discovers the differences in her Sunday world and her weekday world. In **The Widening Circle,** it becomes clear that Ursula is frustrated by her family responsibilities. Ursula is sent to Nottingham High School for Girls as a result. There, open to far more than her parents have ever experienced, she enjoys life and blossoms as she studies Latin, French and Algebra. The next chapter, **First Love,** recounts how before she finishes high school however, her interests are diverted when she meets the young Anton Skrebensky, the son of a Polish friend of her grandmother Lydia, the same boy her parents visited years earlier. Anton is at that time a Lieutenant in the British Army. On a month's leave, he falls in love with Ursula who is already smitten by him. The intense love that she offers him when he returns on his next leave has the effect of driving him off. At a wedding dance, they talk about the war and Skrebensky becomes afraid of what he sees as Ursula's over-possessive love. In the chapter **Shame,** Ursula and Winifred Inger, her school mistress, become involved in a lesbian relationship. Surprisingly though, some time later and because of Ursula, Winifred meets her uncle Tom and eventually marries him.

Then, in the next chapter, **The Man's World,** when she finishes high school, Ursula passes an examination that permits her entry to university. Ursula, always wanting independence, seeks to lessen the financial burden on her parents and decides to teach for a short time to accumulate money to defray the costs of further education. When Ursula mentions the possibility of leaving home, Anna and Will are furious. As a compromise, they help her find a position as a teacher in a local school. Ursula suffers through two frustrating and thankless years at low pay at St. Philip's School in Ilkeston. So by this time, Ursula realizes after trying religion, having responsibility for others, an unsatisfactory first love, and a lesbian affair, that she must concentrate on her own life. In another chapter entitled **The Widening Circle,** the now very large Brangwen family moves to a new house in Beldover. Despite difficulties with her mother, Ursula pours her energy into the move, helps set up the new home, and becomes even more eager to continue her education. Preferring botany over other subjects, Ursula decides to continue her studies at University College in Nottingham in a field she believes will permit her to learn things possessing an absolute truth.

The chapter **The Bitterness of Ecstasy** recounts that around the end of the Boer War, Anton Skrebensky writes Ursula a letter saying that he wishes to see her on his next leave in England. Receiving the letter after six years of separation upsets Ursula, but when Anton arrives, she returns to him with greater intensity than before. During the Easter holiday, Anton and Ursula spend a week at a London hotel where they pass as husband and wife. They go on to Paris and Rouen as soon as Ursula finishes her summer classes. Yet Ursula does not want to marry Anton; instead, she plans to return to finish her degree. Here Lawrence emphasizes the shift in attitudes in this couple in light of the two earlier generations. Where Tom and Lydia represented a mature and responsible couple in comparison to the immaturity and resulting problems between Anna and Will, Anton and Ursula exchange places between emotional and professional goals.

Anton continues to insist on their marriage. He speaks of his Army career and of leaving England to serve in India. During this time, Ursula neglects her studies so much that she fails the final examinations for her degree. This means she must study and take new exams before the end of the summer. When Ursula fails the examinations a second time, Anton presses her to marry him immediately. He argues that as his wife in India her degree or lack of it will make no difference to their life. At this time, they attend a house party where both Ursula and Anton realize that their relationship is not strong enough to make their marriage a success. They leave the party separately. Some weeks later Skrebensky arrives in India where he marries the daughter of his regimental commander.

In the final chapter **The Rainbow,** when Ursula learns that she is pregnant, she decides to write to Anton to tell him of the baby and to ask him to marry her. Before his response arrives, though Ursula has a wild and dangerous encounter with horses running through a field. She falls ill with pneumonia. As a result, she loses the unborn child. One day during her convalescence, Ursula spots a rainbow in the sky, a sign she takes as foretelling better times to come: "She saw in the rainbow the earth's new architecture, the old, brittle corruption of houses and factories swept away, the world built up in a living fabric of Truth, fitting to the over-arching heaven." (459) ✽

List of Characters in
The Rainbow

Tom Brangwen: The youngest of the six children of Alfred Brangwen and "a woman from Heanor" (14), Tom develops into a more responsible and mature young man than his brothers. He happily takes over the running of Marsh Farm at age 18. Tom, a man accustomed to working in open fields, has the self-assurance from an early age that determination and work produce positive results. This trait helps him face the changes taking place in his community and society. His greatest personal challenge is to attain and then maintain his relationship with Lydia.

Lydia Lensky Brangwen: Arriving to the area as a widow, Lydia finds employment and shelter for herself and her young daughter at the vicar's house. In her former marriage, Lydia was used to a more articulate husband and gave herself over to his care when sick. She lost two other children from this marriage before arriving in England. Lydia comes from a higher social class than Tom and is six years older.

Anna Lensky Brangwen: Anna is an uneasy and willful woman, who after being pampered as a child by her stepfather Tom has problems adjusting to others outside the confines of the farm. In Will, she sees an escape from the farm but also finds another person willing to care for her. Anna initially relishes the physical intimacy she shares with Will during their honeymoon. Her thoughts and energy soon shift almost exclusively to motherhood. She gives Will nine children.

William Brangwen: This is Tom Brangwen's nephew who comes to live at Marsh Farm while working at a local factory. Will's passive and deferential character—two qualities that suit Anna immediately—inhibit his ability not only to cope with Anna's demands but also to understand or develop his inner emotions. Outwardly, he expresses his individuality in his wood carvings and his appreciation for church architecture and art.

Ursula Brangwen: The first child of Will and Anna and Will's favorite, Ursula's perspective on life looks outward from the confines of her family. As a young girl, Ursula is uncomfortable when given the responsibility of caring for her siblings. Ursula prefers instead the pleasure of learning that she finds in school. She seeks the truth that this learning can provide and the career and consequent independence that an education offers. Her love for Anton interrupts and jeopardizes her goals, but Ursula, as she recuperates from her severest challenge, gains a new clarity on her life and future.

Gudrun Brangwen: The second daughter of Anna and William, Gudrun stays close to her sister in childhood and develops a keen interest in painting as she grows up.

Anton Skrebensky: Son of Baron Skrebensky—compatriot of and friend to Lydia Lensky Brangwen—Anton meets Ursula when on leave from the Army. Although Anton believes he loves Ursula, in their first encounters Anton shies away from any commitment. ❈

Critical Views on
The Rainbow

LETTER FROM D. H. LAWRENCE TO LADY OTTOLINE MORRELL

[In this letter, Lawrence may have sown the seed later used by Lady Ottoline against him. Lawrence refers here to James Douglas of the *Star* and Clement Shorter of the *Sphere* who both wrote severe reviews against *The Rainbow* in English newspapers of the day. He tells Lady Ottoline that his lawyer has suggested bringing a libel suit against them. She does exactly the same two years later.]

To Lady Ottoline Morrell, from 1 Byron Villas, Hampstead, 3 December 1915

My dear Ottoline: You cannot conceive how dark and hideous London is today, mouldering in a dank fog. I am glad we have let this flat. Even were we staying in England, I should have to leave London.

We were so sorry the flowers were not with the berries, in Oxford, at the station yesterday, and so glad when they came this morning. They are on the table, under your embroidery, which hangs on the wall. It is a great success, in its dark green frame. We love it: it is like a new presence in the house: it gives a new quality to the room: quite new. It is strange.

We had some fine hours, all of us together, didn't we?

This morning Prince Bibesco came to see us. He was rather nice—really concerned about the injustice to *The Rainbow*. But I liked him: his nature is really rather fresh—but not deep. Perhaps in society he is less simple.

Carswell—a new barrister—very much wants to have the case of *The Rainbow* fought out. He says there is a clear and complete case of libel against [James] Douglas and [Clement] Shorter; also he says that acting on Sir John Simon's suggestion, one could have another copy of *The Rainbow* seized, and I could bring the whole matter into court, and have it thrashed out. But my spirit will not rise to it. I can't come so near to them as to fight them. I have done with them. I am not going to pay any more out of my soul, even for the sake of beating them.

We hear of the *Crown de Leon,* a tramp steamer sailing on the 20th of this month, to the West Indies. Probably we shall go by that. It takes a month to reach its destination. But I don't mind that. Heseltine wants to come with us, when we sail, if possible—and failing that as soon after as he can. Suhrawardy also wants to come. . . .

James Douglas, in the *Star,* and Clement Shorter, in the *Sphere,* had written reviews that virtually demanded police prosecution of the author and the publisher of *The Rainbow.*

—D. H. Lawrence, "Letter to Lady Ottoline Morrell." In *The Collected Letters of D. H. Lawrence,* Volume 1, ed. Henry T. Moore (New York: Viking, 1962): pp. 160–162.

Letter from D. H. Lawrence to J. B. Pinker

[*The Rainbow,* like Lawrence's other novels, caused controversy among the critics and the censors as well. Here Lawrence petitions Pinker's help in defending the work and, in passing, asks for money, a constant concern of Lawrence's at this time in his career.]

To J. B. Pinker, from Greatham, Pulborough, Sussex, 23 April 1915

Dear Pinker: Miss Meynell told me you wanted the MS. of the novel. Lady Ottoline Morrell is reading it just now: she will send it on to you as she reads it.

I hope you are willing to fight for this novel. It is nearly three years of hard work, and I am proud of it, and it must be stood up for. I'm afraid there are parts of it Methuen won't want to publish. He must. I will take out sentences and phrases, but I won't take out paragraphs or pages. So you must tell me in detail if there are real objections to printing any parts.

You see a novel, after all this period of coming into being, has a definite organic form, just as a man has when he is grown. And we don't ask a man to cut his nose off because the public don't like it: because he must have a nose, and his own nose, too.

Oh God, I hope I'm not going to have a miserable time over this book, now I've at last got it pretty much to its real being.

Very soon I shall have no money. I got £25 paid in the last time at the last moment. Now it is nearly gone. I depend on you to get me something.

>—D. H. Lawrence, "Letter to J. B. Pinker." In *The Collected Letters of D. H. Lawrence,* Volume 1, ed. Henry T. Moore (New York: Viking, 1962): 160–162.

Diane S. Bonds on D. H. Lawrence's Literary Inheritors

> [Professor Bonds has served on the editorial board of *The D. H. Lawrence Review* and is the author of *Language and the Self in D. H. Lawrence* (1987). This essay's point of departure is Joyce Carol Oates' critical works on Lawrence including *The Hostile Sun: The Poetry of D. H. Lawrence* (1973) and her essay on *Women in Love*. It is Professor Bonds' belief that Oates' own creative work exhibits considerable influence from Lawrence. In the excerpt, Bonds illustrates textual connections between *The Rainbow* and Oates' work *them* (1969).]

The unmistakable echoes of *The Rainbow* in *them* indicate the points of thematic intersection between Lawrence and Oates. In both novels, characters oscillate between a longing for some 'surety' or 'fixity', some stability of the self, and a longing for change, for mobility, for self-transcendence. Jules Wendall's mother, Loretta, carries within her 'a forlorn sensation . . . , rising often, out of melancholy and weary joy, that everyone who was born must be a person—one person only—and that this personal, private, nameless kernel of the self could neither be broken down nor escaped from . . . '. The kernel metaphor, so important in *The Rainbow*, bears an irony in both Oates and Lawrence: while the 'hard unkillable selfish kernel of Being' would seem to promise some stability, its confines, on the one hand, produce a powerful longing for self-transcendence in characters, and yet, on the other, are often insufficient to create a sense of permanence and substantiality as a self. Loretta, like Tom Brangwen, feels 'unsure and unfixed', 'so unestablished': '. . . nothing permanent had really happened to her. She had thought certain things were permanent, fixing her, but she had been mistaken. . . . Nothing had fixed her yet'.

In both novels, characters seek both permanence for the self and transcendence of the ego through sexual relationships or erotic experience. Lawrence's novel implicitly asks how the momentaneous verification by the impersonal, a verification derived almost solely through sexual consummation in his works, wears over time. What is the effect or power of fourth-dimensional experience in the three-dimensional world? Oates's novel might be taken to pose the same question, but framing it in a context where daily interactions are informed by violence or the threat of violence. As we might expect, the results are even more equivocal than in Lawrence's novel, which, as Eugene Goodheart has put it, communicates a 'sense of the *inadequacy* of the loves' that is 'somewhat puzzling' given 'the transcendent nature of the consummations'.

One of the primary ways in which Oates's novel tests the Lawrentian hypothesis is through the literalization of the key Lawrentian metaphor of baptism by fire, as if implicitly to level the criticism that Lawrence's exploration is far too figurative. Early in *them* we encounter a 'baptism by fire' more literal than the fire of Paul Morel's sexual experience with Clara Dawes. After witnessing the gruesome and fiery aftermath of a plane crash, the child Jules becomes fascinated with the transformative power of fire—so much so that he ends up burning down the family barn. Although he is brutally punished ('You'll wind up in the electric chair and I'll pull the switch!' screams his grandmother in a prophecy echoed later by a nun in the parochial school he attends in Detroit), fire becomes, in Jules's imagination, associated with expansion, transformation, 'breaking out' and realizing the 'great value' of his 'true essence'— that is, with his view of himself as 'pure spirit struggling to break free'. When, as an adolescent, he reads 'about a man from India named Vinoba Bhave', who claims, 'Fire burns and does its duty', he is inspired to the thought that he would like 'not to be a saint exactly but to live a secular life parallel to a sacred life—a modern life, at all costs—to expand Jules out to the limits of his skin and the range of his eyesight'.

> —Diane S. Bonds, "Joyce Carol Oates: Testing the Lawrentian Hypothesis." In *D. H. Lawrence's Literary Inheritors.* Ed. Keith Cushman and Dennis Jackson, Macmillan, 1991.

Elaine Feinstein on Lawrence's Women

[Professor Feinstein, author of many scholarly works including *Lady Chatterley's Confession* (1995), examines the private life of D. H. Lawrence. In this literary biography, Feinstein attempts to connect episodes from his works to Lawrence's life. In this excerpt, she suggests parallels in the relationships the women in *The Rainbow* have with their men to the real-life relation between Lawrence and his wife Frieda.]

The novel we now know as *The Rainbow* was written between August 1914 and May 1915, after a third draft of 'The Sisters' (called 'The Wedding Ring') had been rejected by Methuen as too frank to be publishable. The life between Lawrence and Frieda flowed into the new novel, and Lawrence was proud of the autobiographical source of the work. He had been quite properly teased by Frieda for his depiction of Clara Dawes, who leaves her husband only to return to him, in *Sons and Lovers,* and he determined to put that right by showing women like Frieda as confidently in control of their own lives. He felt ambiguously about that confidence, however, and confessed another intention: to show Frieda 'in her Godalmightiness in all its glory'.

Lawrence needed to believe in the health of the marriage he and Frieda had made. They were capable of the most intense happiness together (as a record of such happiness *The Rainbow* is almost unequalled), so he was prepared to accept the raging quarrels that so dismayed his friends, and even to insist they had moral value. But these quarrels were no longer only about Frieda's lament for her lost children. There was another, more intensely felt dynamic, and the novel explores its source.

Set between Nottinghamshire and Derbyshire and spanning three generations, from the Industrial Revolution to the First World War, *The Rainbow* has a traditional novelistic shape. There is no one character that Lawrence identifies with as he had with Paul Morel in *Sons and Lovers* (though Tom Brangwen, at the heart of the first part of the novel, is described as 'mardy' like Lawrence, and suffers from the same awed and anxious feelings about women); what matters is that every male in the book is given a pattern of feelings which resembles Lawrence's relation to Frieda. On Tom's first sight of the Polish Mrs Lensky (whom Lawrence names Lydia, after his mother), he immediately recognises the woman he wants. 'That's her,' he exclaims. Like Frieda, Mrs. Lensky is well-born and self-possessed, has already been married, and is six years older than Tom. These attributes free Tom from his usual sexual anxiety, and make him feel confident enough to ask Mrs Lensky to marry him.

Mrs Lensky has a mysterious separateness which contributes to her sexual charm; she often seems to ignore Tom (as Miriam never could ignore Paul Morel), and there is a mixture of fear and worship in his desire. He is no longer afraid his passion will soil her (as he had felt with local girls), but as the relationship deepens he comes to be maddened by that separateness, which rouses him to raging fury.

There is nothing imaginary about the separateness that threatens him once Lydia becomes pregnant. Then he speaks of feeling 'deposed', as if the only place he had were being taken away by a child. Indeed, Lydia's daughter by her first husband does try to oust Tom from her bed. Tom's jealousy (rather like Lawrence's quivering hatred whenever Frieda expressed her longing for her children) is presented as an overwhelming need for attention. At one point he reflects: 'He would smash her into attention.' Nevertheless, the description of Tom's relationship to his stepchild has rarely been matched; the tenderness with which Tom carries the sobbing child into a lantern-lit, warm-smelling cowshed while Anna is giving birth is imagined memorably:

> He opened the doors, upper and lower, and they entered into the high, dry barn that smelled warm, even if it were not warm. He hung the lantern on the nail and shut the door. They were in another world now. The light shed softly on the timbered barn, on the white-washed walls, and the great heap of hay; instruments cast their shadows largely, a ladder rose to the dark arch of a loft. Outside there was the driving rain, inside the softly-illuminated stillness and calmness of the barn.
> Holding the child on one arm, he set about preparing the food for the cows, filling a pan with chopped hay and brewers' grain and a little meal. The child, all wonder, watched what he did. A new being was created in her for the new conditions. Sometimes, a little spasm, eddying from the bygone storm of sobbing, shook her small body. Her eyes were wide and wondering, pathetic ...
> There was a noise of chains running as the cows lifted or dropped their heads sharply; then a contented soothing sound, a long snuffing as the beasts ate in silence.
> The journey had to be performed several times. There was the rhythmic sound of the shovel in the barn, then the man returned walking stiffly between the two weights, the face of the child peering out from the shawl. Then the next time, as he stooped, she freed her arm and put it round his neck, clinging soft and warm, making all easier.
> The beasts fed, he dropped the pan and sat down on a box, to arrange the child.
> 'Will the cows go to sleep now?' she said, catching her breath as she spoke.

As the marriage develops Tom has to learn to make do with less sex than he wants, and it may be that Lawrence was already having to do the same; perhaps, like Lydia Lensky, Frieda only wanted her husband in her own way and to her own measure. For her part, Lydia complains that Tom needs her excessively, and does not do enough to make her love him. It is hard to see how Lawrence could have done more for Frieda: he earned all the money, attracted all the friends, and did all the housework; Lydia's accusation, in my view, nevertheless arose from Lawrence's own experience, and relates to the amount of pleasure he gave Frieda in bed. With another author this would be an unwarrantable conjecture, but Lawrence's later writing, with its condemnation of foreplay and disgust at women who seek too greedily for their own sexual satisfaction, makes the speculation legitimate. In any case, his quarrels with Frieda were by now openly about their sexual relationship. During the autumn of 1914, Murry and Lawrence had many long and intimate conversations about sex; partly because the Lawrences' public quarrels invited it. On one occasion Murry heard Frieda accuse Lawrence of taking her 'as a dog does a bitch', and there were angry words which suggested Frieda no longer wanted Lawrence sexually in any way.

—Elaine Feinstein, *Lawrence's Women: The Intimate Life of D. H. Lawrence* (New York: HarperCollins Publishers, 1993): pp. 126–128.

Mark Kinkead-Weekes on the Exploratory Imagination of D. H. Lawrence

[Kinkead-Weekes is the author of *D. H. Lawrence: Triumph to Exile, 1912–1922* (1996) and the editor of the Cambridge edition of *The Rainbow*. In this extensive essay, Professor Kinkead-Weekes considers the evolution of texts that ended in the production of *The Rainbow* and *Women in Love*. Kinkead-Weekes believes it important to factor into their creation the effort that Lawrence also put into two non-fiction works: *Study of Thomas Hardy* and *The Crown* (1915). This excerpt focuses on the Cathedral scene in *The Rainbow* and the connection in spiritual themes to the *Study of Thomas Hardy*, a work not published until 1932.]

The evolution of one of *The Rainbow*'s greatest scenes, the episode in Lincoln Cathedral, will show how the imaginative exploration grows out of the *Study*. At a very late stage in composition, moreover, the novel remains fluid in Lawrence's imagination, which finds it necessary to move on, by its own kind of 'logic', to a stage quite beyond the scope of the treatise.

The Cathedral scene was not in *The Wedding Ring*, since we can watch Lawrence in the first draft of *The Rainbow* struggling to get hold of it, and failing at first. He had grasped the contrast between the marriage of Tom and Lydia and the young married life of Anna and Will, and had summed it up in terms of his dominant image: in one case, the pillar of fire and the pillar of cloud locked into an arch, creating freedom, and a gateway to the beyond; in the other, the rich woman possessing her husband, settled on Pisgah, still within sight of the rainbow and the promised land, but capable only of being a threshold from which her children can set forth, because she has conquered.

Lawrence must have felt, however, that he needed to explore the religious dimension of the marriage further, beyond merely personal relationship—even when 'personal' is defined at the depth of a chapter like 'Anna Victrix'. In the *Study*, as part of a long account of the spiritual dialectic in art, he had briefly remarked on the mediaeval cathedrals:

> The worship of Europe, predominantly female, all through the mediaeval period, was to the male, to the incorporeal Christ, as a bridegroom, whilst the art produced was the collective, stupendous emotional gesture of the Cathedrals, where a blind collective impulse rose into concrete form. It was the profound, sensuous desire and gratitude which produced an art of architecture, whose essence is in utter stability, of movement resolved and centralized, of absolute movement, that has no relationship with any other form, that admits the existence of no other form, but is conclusive, propounding in its sum the One Being of All.
>
> There was, however, in the Cathedrals, already the denial of the Monism which the Whole uttered. All the little figures, the gargoyles, the imps, the human faces, whilst subordinated within the Great Conclusion of the Whole, still, from their obscurity, jeered their mockery of the Absolute, and declared for multiplicity, polygeny.

Lawrence's first attempt to realize this within the response of his human characters was, as one might expect, rather gushing and repetitive, allowing his imagination free rein. Will's response is a good deal longer than it is now, aiming again and again at the same target. The church is a great darkness and silence, a 'dark rainbow', a 'link of darkness' between the eternity before birth and the eternity after death. It is 'away from time, always away from life'. The repetition is not however merely repetitive; for Lawrence tries to create a succession of passionate leapings up from the 'plain earth' to the 'stud of ecstasy' at the roof, that point of tension where the 'immemorial darkness' is both thrust up, and weighs back—again, and again, and again as the eye passes down the nave towards the 'other mystery' of the altar.

In the same manuscript, he revised extensively with a new conception. Now the church is not outside life, it is the womb within which all life is implicit. Light begins to enter, a twilight, yet 'the embryo of all light'. The church lies

> like a seed in silence, dark before germination, silenced after death. Containing birth and death, potential with all the noise and transition of life, the cathedral remained hushed, a great involved seed whereof the flower would be radiant life inconceivable, but whose beginning and whose end lay in the two extremes of silence. Like a shadowy rainbow, the jewelled gloom spanned from silence to silence, darkness to darkness, fecundity to fecundity, as a seed spans from life to life and death to death, containing the secret of all folded between its parts.

He cut about a page and a half, began to discipline, condense, heighten.

The more significant growth however is in the response of Anna. We can tell little about the first version, since all but a few sentences were deleted and replaced when Lawrence revised Will's response, but 'she too was overcome', though she resisted. In revision, she is at first carried away almost as much as Will; only she is not fulfilled. For her soul longs to 'be cast at last on the threshold of the unknown', at the altar, but always she is made to leap 'to the ecstasy and the isolation and the agony up there'. That night, she becomes increasingly dissatisfied, seeing the experience as a kind of crucifixion of self-knowledge. And again she longs for the march of the great pillars down the nave to the threshold of the unknown. She dreams of angels, flaming in praise around the presence of God. But when they go back to the cathedral the next day, there is no getting beyond self-realization, no transfiguration of the stigmata of self-knowledge, no door to the beyond. She is shut in. Even if she thinks of the smallness of man's ego against the 'whole rotunda of day or the dome of night' there is no help, for 'which star should she choose?' In the cathedral the altar is 'a dragged nest, the Mystery was gone'. She longs to take off like a bird, 'to rise into the gladness of light . . . to escape from the builded earth, from man's day after day.

Was man and his present measure to be forever the measure of the universe? But she must grasp at some resistance before she could thrust off. It was so difficult.' So she grasps at the little faces.

> —Mark Kinkead-Weekes, "The Marble and the Statue: The Exploratory Imagination of D. H. Lawrence." In *D. H. Lawrence: Critical Assessments.* Ed. David Ellis and Ornella di Zordo (Helm Information Ltd., 1992).

Henry Miller on the World of Lawrence

> [Miller, the noted and, in his own right, controversial American writer and author of *The Tropic of Cancer*—among other canonical works—draws on an episode in *The Rainbow* to express his admiration. Here Henry Miller cites the episode in *The Rainbow* when Ursula and Anton experience violent passion together. Miller suggests that the extreme tone surrounding their joining may be deliberately done by Lawrence in an effort to eke more out of the episode as well as out of life. According to Miller, the intensity of Lawrence's "sex-crucified" genius is a soul-struggle like that of Ursula with Anton. (Miller refers to John Middleton Murry here.)]

Truth demands that, in interpreting a man's life, the emphasis should be on the predominant characteristic of his nature, which in the case of Lawrence was the virility of his creative power, a power which certainly overshadowed any sexual or personal insufficiency, assuming that there was such. To analyze Lawrence then according to a formula, to attempt to organize by logic that superb chaos which he was, is to leave out the most important Lawrence—the dreamer and creator. Because of his very physical weakness, and his struggle against it, certain things were revealed to Lawrence which were concealed from other men; but to emphasize this weakness rather than the importance of the revelation is to be untrue to the creative dreams which were as much a part of the man as his human life. Take for example that passage in *The Rainbow* wherein Lawrence describes the union between Anton and Ursula, a passage which

Murry's scientific dissection characterizes as a revelation of Lawrence's "animality." We are informed that it is a description of the disintegration which results from this "animality." Murry concludes that Lawrence's own terrible experience of self-immolation in the sexual experience left him unsatisfied because he was too weak to achieve satisfaction. But there may be quite another "explanation" of this violent union between Anton and Ursula. This devastating conflict might also be regarded, not as a mere sexual phenomenon, but as the creator's craving for a climax far bigger than the climaxes which life has to offer. It might well be a creative voraciousness beside which the average man's hunger is insignificant. More life! More hunger! More pain! More experience! And not just quantitative experience, but qualitative experience—intensity of experience.

This overwhelming urge for experience, this fierce, devouring hunger for life, it is true, generally costs the artist his life. His is divided between, at one and at the same time, the desire to live out his deepest impulses and to preserve himself from the destruction which must inevitably ensue. The fear of ultimate physical extinction leads him to immortalize himself through art. His experience of life consequently comes to be regarded by him as both a necessary ailment and an evil, destructive thing. And since it is the sexual life which, as for most of us, provides the greatest measure of experience and suffering, the symbolic, imaginative derivatives of that life endow his art-product with the most cruel and poignant outlines of feeling.

Just as he glorifies life, in order to slay it through his art, so he glorifies woman in order to execrate her; punish her, for the necessitous character of her role, which he himself recognizes only too clearly. It is because his creative instinct is so strong that he is obliged to deny, at least in his art, the tyranny of her power. *Son of Woman* he is, but it is as *Father* that he endows himself for his role in life. Born a mortal he craves immortality; born of woman he appoints himself begetter. Not of her are his children produced, but of HIM who is all. He looks to her for his experience only in order to achieve his final isolation. The sex act is not the consummation or the fulfillment—it is the point of departure. But it is just because his hunger is sharper, his need of experience more exigent, that his thirst for fulfillment, for an isolated union with the universe, emerges with such a painful, discordant clarity.

The fulfillment which Lawrence depicts in *Lady Chatterley's Lover* is not the fulfillment of the artist. It is in *The Rainbow* that we witness this devastating, harrowing soul-struggle. And the struggle has a "disintegrating" character simply because it is an unequal struggle. That which the woman is terrified of, the urgent quest for something beyond her, which makes a real union forever impossible, that is the sole preoccupation of the artist, because it is his problem, his conflict. No mortal woman will ever satisfy the demands of this demon. No mortal man either. That is why love, marriage, friendship, all prove to be insufficient, added tortures to his existence.

God be praised that life can still throw out now and then such an abnormal, diseased, sex-crucified, sex-sodden genius as Lawrence. A fine affair it will be when all the neurotics have been analyzed, when all men have been made "normal" (which is a contradiction in essence), when the lion lies down with the lamb and there is no more struggle, no more conflict, no more pain, only bread and butter for everybody and peace on earth and stinking good-will towards men.

I trust it is clear by this time that I am not writing a "criticism" of Lawrence. This is an appreciation, passionate and prejudiced, an emotional document, which I consider the only kind of criticism worth while.

—Henry Miller, *The World of Lawrence: A Passionate Appreciation* (Santa Barbara: Capra Press, 1980): pp. 53–55.

Paul Poplawski on Creativity and the Religious Impulse

[Professor Poplawski, from Trinity College Carmarthen in Wales, is also the author of *D. H. Lawrence: A Reference Companion* (1996). In this work, Poplawski presents an examination of Lawrence's concept of creativity in relation to his religious beliefs. In this excerpt from his chapter "*The Rainbow* II: Rhythms of the Unknown God," Professor

[Poplawski contends that Lawrence exploits rhythms of prose to expose the psychology of his characters. Here Poplawski elucidates his point by highlighting biblical allusions in the text.]

Apart from overtly mimetic uses of rhythm to evoke the "whirlpool" of psychological states, there is also a distinct structural rhythm operating within *The Rainbow*. The narrative develops according to a regular internal pattern that both establishes the novel's overall shape and creates an increasingly resonant rhythm to counterpoint and complement the more immediate rhythms of individual sections of the book. This pattern is constructed partly out of the tripartite development of the dramatic action and partly out of the various sequences of the novel's symbolism. Peter Balbert clearly articulates the nature of the former part of the pattern when he writes that the tripartite structure of the novel

> can be regarded as a series of three concentric and open-ended circles, with the Marsh Canal as convenient connecting point in the center. . . . Each circle is open-ended because the literal and metaphorical birth of one generation moves eventually into that of the other—and only after the similar cycles of psychological concerns that aid or retard the birth have been described with the similar rhythmic use of metaphor, syntax, and incident.

The construction of the plot in this way, upon three closely connected generations, establishes a pattern of recapitulation and gradual creative growth, in which past wisdom and experience are slowly augmented and transformed into new ideas and impulses. It creates, further, a sense of organic communal development and progress, and it deepens the sense of purpose and meaning in the individual lives that are presented to us.

Another constituent pattern of the novel's structural rhythm, which similarly accentuates the solemnity of the characters' experiences, is the pattern of biblical allusion and symbol. In the very nature of the Brangwens' experiences, and in the epic tone in which these are portrayed, there lies a clear parallel with the style, rhythm, and structure of the stories of the Old Testament. Most obviously, the novel opens in the style of Genesis, and it ends with its own version of Revelation. In between, there are constant references to the Bible and to sacred Christian doctrine, and the pattern of events themselves often has a certain deliberate portentousness evocative of biblical narrative. The fact that much of the symbolism in the novel comes from Genesis and Revelation underpins the way that the novel develops from the early germination of a "blood-intimate" Brangwen spirit to Ursula's final revelatory vision of "a new germination."

Seen individually, the many biblical allusions in the novel gain their meaning by a process of adaptation in which their biblical significance leads into or underscores a more important dramatic meaning that is wholly unrelated to the Bible. They are often used in this way to emphasize aspects of a character's nature or development, as, for example, in the case of Will's association, through his wood-carving, with Eve. The biblical associations of first beginnings and of creation are channeled by Lawrence toward representing the beginning of Will's love for Anna, his creativity in carpentry, and his deep-rooted, naive Christian faith. The fact that he never finishes the carving and eventually burns it therefore has a clear symbolic significance in our understanding of Will's finally unfulfilled character. Similarly, Ursula's identification with the biblical vision of the Sons of God coming to take to wife the daughters of men comes to symbolize not her Christian reverence but her profound yearning for such a visionary experience within her own actual life. More general symbols such as the rainbow and the horses at the end of the book equally derive some of their significance from their biblical origins, but Lawrence's rainbow promises an earthly form of fulfillment unrelated to the biblical covenant between God and man, and his horses too symbolize aspects of a distinctly corporeal revelation.

Perhaps most importantly, the use of biblical symbolism in *The Rainbow* should be seen as a whole, as a unified device that serves to heighten the epic quality of the novel in general, and of the characters' experiences in particular, and to emphasize that we are to recognize both as being quintessentially "religious." Looked at in this way, the symbolism cleverly accentuates the dramatic conflict played out within the novel between a traditional predetermined religious response to life, which is portrayed as stultifying, and the more spontaneous, individually-fashioned response that is represented as profoundly life-enhancing and therefore religious in Lawrence's sense. Lawrence, as it were, "deconstructs" the biblical symbolism he makes use of, and in doing so transforms almost an entire myth in the process of forging his own new one—his new metaphysic of creativity.

> —Paul Poplawski, *Promptings of Desire: Creativity and the Religious Impulse in the Works of D. H. Lawrence* (London: Greenwood Press, 1993): pp. 106–108.

Jack Stewart on Vision and Expression

> [Professor Stewart has written extensively on Lawrence's novels and his affinity for art, and is also the editor of *Michael Bullock: Selected works* (1998). The present work studies Lawrence's concept of vision as expressed in visual perception and ontological vision and the writer's combination of visual arts and writing in his fiction. In his chapter on *The Rainbow*, Stewart explains that Expressionism "involves empathy and abstraction" (52) to explain the echoes of artistic periods, such as Renaissance art, English landscape painting, and French Impressionism, found in Lawrence's work. In this excerpt, Professor Stewart discusses the Cathedral scene in the context of Expressionism.]

As Will and Anna approach the spiritual womb of the cathedral, he becomes aware of his own life, suspended at a point of "transitation" ("the action of passing, passage" [OED]) between the darkness before birth and the darkness after death. Entering the cathedral, he "enter[s] the twilight of both darknesses, the hush of the two-fold silence, where dawn was sunset, and the beginning and the end were one." Will becomes aware that extremes of being contain contraries; in his epiphany in the cathedral, he participates in a mystic marriage of light and darkness. The luminous language is fraught with oxymorons and opposites coupled in Taoistic embrace: "east and west," "dawn and sunset," beginning and end, "coloured darkness," "jewelled gloom," "music upon silence," "light upon darkness," "fecundity upon death," "the root and the flower," "'before' and 'after.'" Will's visionary rite of passage recalls Wordsworth's crossing of the Alps:

> Tumult and peace, the darkness and the light—
> Were all like workings of one mind, the features
> Of the same face, blossoms upon one tree;
> Characters of the great Apocalypse,
> The types and symbols of Eternity,
> Of first, and last, and midst, and without end.
> (*Prelude*, Book 6, ll. 635–40)

Apocalyptic symbolism in "The Cathedral" is crossed with primitivism and expressionism. Through projection and empathy, Will fuses his spiritual drive with architectural forms in a kind of Gothic animism. Most remarkable are the concentration and vitalism of the language, that make the passage not just a mystical excursus but also a ritual enactment, moving in intensifying stages toward the spiritual climax of "one-ing." The excitement and driving rhythms stem from attraction and interpenetration of mutually implicated opposites.

Spiritually, Will achieves oneness with the Cathedral, his soul "at the apex of the arch, clinched in the timeless ecstasy, consummated." But the cultural form is a limitation, and his inspiration is undercut by Anna's skepticism. Against the centrifugal drive of her being toward open sky, his drive is revealed as centripetal, falling back on itself, enclosed within inorganic form. While his vision has intensity, the ironic framing shows it to be incomplete, solipsistic, spiritually onanistic. Will's spirit needs to be married to Anna's sensual drive, or erotic energy will be displaced and inspiration remain unfruitful. His vision of oneness is the substanceless pattern, or ghost, of the Rainbow fusion of spirit and senses, Gothic and Norman, vertical and horizontal, heaven and earth, within a fulfilled form of living. The "third thing" that emerges from this spiritual/material dialectic is radiance—the reader's sense of vital creative vision. Through cumulative phrasing, incremental repetition, and oxymoronic images, Lawrence's language conveys simultaneous but opposing impulses of movement and poise, flow and concentration, kinesis and stasis. It is dynamic, expressing tension of opposites ("clinched") rather than resolution ("consummated"). The kinetic emphasis falls on *desire* for harmony rather than its achievement. Abstraction and empathy are well matched, but assertion of the ideal outdoes realization. The "perfect, swooning consummation, the timeless ecstasy" cannot be sustained in time, especially when body and spirit are sundered as in Will's and Anna's marriage. The very intensity of Will's striving hints at willful sublimation; not surprisingly, Anna resents his stealing fire from their marriage. His vision lacks substance, because it depends upon the "neutrality" of conflicting drives rather than their "consummation" in a genuine marriage of opposites.

Expressionist dynamism and abstraction—the colorful cornucopia of symbols and pulsing, mimetic rhythms—deepen the reader's experience. There is a sense, in "The Cathedral," of dim symbols, momentarily illuminated, overarching and overshadowing individual existence. The passage is an attempt to express the "inner necessity" of Will's spirit, that of a religious artist, in which "coloured darkness" produces "spiritual vibration," and its structural symmetries and luminous images recall the dreamlike style of *Der Blaue Reiter* (Marc, Macke, Kandinsky, and Feininger). "The Cathedral" combines symbolism with expressionism; ideas come alive and the tension of Will's being is expressed in inspired vision. Lawrence's empathy with spiritual dynamics does not, of course, mean that his vision is limited by the character's, as Anna's conflicting viewpoint shows. But expressionism reveals the conflict and yearning for fulfillment in Will in a way that realism could never do. Lawrence's style projects Will's inner being into the interplay between abstract "form-harmony" (Kandinsky) and concrete sensuousness. Here expressionism, animating symbolism, conveys an "abstract-whole" that could not be suggested by the most faithful mimesis. Will's sublime, all-encompassing experience is objectively placed as the phenomenon of a being in transit. His spirit animates stone, transforming it into a symbol of aspiration. But, for Anna, "God burned no more in that bush." Will and Anna represent dialectically opposed spiritual and material drives, and the novel presents the "trembling instability of the balance."

—Jack Stewart, *The Vital Art of D. H. Lawrence: Vision and Expression* (Carbondale: Southern Illinois University Press, 1999): pp. 59–62.

Plot Summary of
Women in Love

(Textual quotations are from Lawrence, D. H. *Women in Love*. New York: Penguin, 2000.)

Lawrence entitled the first draft of this work *The Sisters*, begun in early 1913, and worked on a second draft in the late summer. A third draft, called *The Wedding Ring*, had elements of both *The Rainbow* and *Women in Love*. Lawrence returned to the parts corresponding to what we know today as *Women in Love* in April 1916. Further revisions took place from then until September 1919. The work was published in New York by Seltzer in 1920, providing Lawrence finally with some financial stability.

In the opening chapter, **Sisters,** Lawrence introduces Ursula Brangwen, a 26-year-old teacher, and her sister Gudrun, 25, recently returned from several years in a London art school. Ursula is bored by the dreariness of her surroundings and Gudrun finds the adjustment to village life depressing. They discuss their views on marriage and walk to the village church to 'look at' a wedding. Lawrence here and throughout the text, focuses on their clothing—the colors, the fabric, its texture—which sharply contrast with the dullness of the mining community. The two sisters watch as the bridal party and the guests arrive at the church for the Crich daughter's wedding. From her stay in London, Gudrun recognizes many of the other guests, including Hermione Roddice who arrives with Rupert Birkin, a school supervisor known to Ursula. The young women listen as their father plays the church organ. Gerald, the oldest Crich son, makes a lasting impression on Gudrun.

The Crich family is the focus in **Shortlands.** The wedding reception takes place on the grounds of the family estate. Gerald, as oldest, is host. Gerald and Birkin have the first of many debates on love. Then in **Class Room,** Ursula receives an unexpected visit to her class room from Birkin. Hermione has joined him uninvited and it becomes clear that a rivalry between the two women has been established with Birkin as their target. Hermione debates with Birkin aggressively. Merely witnessing the conversation makes Ursula ill. A walk to Willey Water, the lake near Shortlands, gives Ursula and Gudrun a chance to discuss Gerald and the accidental death of his brother in the chapter called **Diver.** They also concur that Hermione is an impudent bore.

Lawrence continues to develop his view of the relationship between Gerald and Birkin in the next chapter, **In the Train.** Birkin reveals that his goal is to find and stay with one woman. Gerald listens but doubts whether this would suit his own lifestyle. They plan to meet later in London. In **Crême de Menthe,** Lawrence uses a night club in London as the setting for introducing the chic set. Gerald and Birkin meet there and find Miss Darrington, nicknamed 'the Pussum', who whines non-stop and pronounces her r's like w's. She seduces Gerald openly even though Julius Halliday, her former lover and the father of her unborn child, is present. The group moves on to an apartment where Gerald and Birkin are distracted by provocative West African wood-carvings. In **Fetish,** the group dynamics at the apartment take on a more erotic, sometimes homoerotic, tone. Initially all revel in walking about naked. Eventually, Gerald quarrels with Halliday and leaves, not unaware though that Miss Darrington has managed to recapture Halliday.

The scene shifts to Hermione's family estate **Breadalby** where the Brangwen sisters join Gerald and Birkin. Again Lawrence capitalizes on a description of the girls' clothes to favor them over Hermione. The men go swimming and afterwards debate whether women can be 'free agents'. (102) Hermione, true to form, interjects her opinion and Birkin lashes out. Then a contrite Birkin visits Hermione in her rooms. He leaves the house after Hermione attacks him and retreats to the wood where he strips himself naked of clothes and of his problems, preferring instead to roll about in the flora and feel it caress his body.

In **Coal-Dust,** Lawrence constructs a scene of violence and domination for both women to witness. By chance, after school, they see Gerald at the train station mounted on his Arabian mare. The horse is spooked by the noise of the train and rears. Gerald beats the mare into submission causing Gudrun to become hysterical. A darkness and contempt fall over her that will reappear in later confrontations. A sharp contrast in scene and temperament begins **Sketch-Book.** The two sisters are sketching at the lake when they are noticed by Hermione and Gerald. Gudrun catches Gerald observing her and senses a power over him. In **An Island,** Ursula walks on and finds Birkin at a nearby mill house. They talk about love and Ursula concludes that love is a disease for Birkin from which he seeks no cure. Their burgeoning relationship meets its usual obstacle in **Carpeting,** when Hermione shows up at the mill with Gerald. Birkin is furnishing new rooms there which he has invited Ursula to see. Hermione declares that she is there to help, but both Ursula and Birkin believe differently and realize then that Ursula is committed to a battle against Hermione. In the chapter **Mino,** named for the stray cat Birkin finds, the new rooms are furnished and Birkin invites Ursula and Gudrun to see them. Ursula goes alone and is struck by Birkin's unexpected candidness about primal desire. But once piqued, Ursula only wants to hear Birkin make the classic declaration. His guarded words say much more: "Let love be enough then. —I love you then—I love you. I'm bored by the rest." (156)

In a shift of action and focus, **Water-Party** centers on the elder Mr. Crich's annual party at the lake. Gudrun and Ursula attend but row to an island to avoid the other guests. There, they come upon grazing cattle. Gudrun begins to dance among them. Gerald finds her in time to ward off the herd. They talk and in playful defiance Gudrun slaps Gerald across the face. The purportedly innocent blow prophesizes future events. When Gerald acknowledges she has struck the first blow, Gudrun responds: "And I shall strike the last. He was silent. He did not contradict her." (173) But the party turns tragic when Diana Crich, the bride whose wedding Ursula and Gudrun watched, drowns with her young husband. Gerald's physical prowess and efforts to save the couple make a great impression on Gudrun. In **Sunday Evening,** the bereavement continues but Lawrence focuses instead on Ursula's depression over her life. Her gloom provokes what she recognizes as an irrational hatred for Birkin, yet she cannot shake off the misery. The object of her hatred is the center of the next chapter, **Man to Man,** where Lawrence expands on what is the third couple in the text: Birkin and Gerald. Birkin was ill, physically and also sickened by his life. While laid up, he meditates on the lack of importance sex holds for him over the necessity for a 'conjunction' (205) of pure beings in a relationship with one woman. But which? Gerald comes to visit and admits to himself that he really does love Birkin though he does not quite believe in the exaggerations of his life philosophy. They discuss many issues: Ursula and Gudrun, Gerald's youngest sister, Winifred, and their school experiences when Birkin suggests that they make a blood bond. As he leaves, Gerald puts him off: "The eyes of the two men met again. Gerald's, that were keen as a hawk's were suffused now with warm light and with unadmitted love, Birkin looked back as out of the darkness, unsounded and unknown . . ." (216)

In **The Industrial Magnate,** Lawrence steps back from action to provide background information on the Crich family. The family has yet to recover fully from the loss of the drowned daughter. The elder Mr. Crich is dying. Despite many years of marriage, he is frightened by his wife whose relationship with her husband has always been destructive. Mr. Crich has come to depend on Gerald and to favor his youngest, Winifred. Gerald feels the weight of his responsibilities as his father's health worsens. Gudrun accepts an invitation from the elder Mr. Crich in the next chapter, **Rabbit,** to give Winifred drawing lessons. Gudrun suspects that Gerald is behind this plan which for her equates to consenting to be his lover. Winifred is a bright child who responds favorably to Gudrun. When they attempt to play with Winifred's rabbit, Gerald must step in to subdue the animal and in turn becomes more drawn to Gudrun.

After some time, Ursula sees Birkin by chance as he contemplates the moon one evening in **Moony.** Dazzled by the sight, she watches, unnoticed, as he throws stones at the moon. Finally, they talk and kiss at last, but Birkin only wants a passionless 'communion' for the present. The next day, however, he goes to the Brangwen home to announce to her parents that he plans to marry Ursula. She reacts violently to what she considers his bullying tactics. Birkin flees from the confrontation and in **Gladitorial** seeks out Gerald's company and counsel. He confesses that he needs to hit something and suggests they wrestle. After dismissing the servants, the two disrobe and wrestle in front of the fireplace. Their bodies, gleaming with the sweat, meet in the struggle. Lawrence's description of their contact is wholly physical: "Often, in the white, interlaced knot of violent living being that swayed silently, there was no head to be seen, only the swift, tight limbs, the solid white backs, the physical junction of two bodies clinched into oneness." (280)

In **Threshold,** on her return from London, Gudrun accepts the dying Mr. Crich's offer to work with Winifred on the estate. Gerald and Gudrun both feel a desire for passion but continue their restraint. Birkin joins them. To Gudrun's considerable surprise, Gerald blurts out the news of Birkin's impending wedding and mocks him for it. The wedding is the subject of **Woman to Woman.** Birkin has invited Gudrun and Ursula to tea but Hermione shows up first to an empty house since Birkin is otherwise detained. When Ursula arrives, Hermione asks her disarmingly about the engagement. Ursula's expressions of doubt is an open invitation for Hermione, asserting that she is the only woman who truly understands Birkin. The two women continue their verbal sparring until Birkin appears.

Hermione successfully undermines and isolates the furious Ursula in his presence. In **Excurse**, Birkin seeks Ursula out after the confrontation by Hermione. Birkin gives Ursula three rings: an opal, a sapphire, and a topaz. Inwardly, Ursula experiences great pleasure from his gift, but this is short-lived when, on their drive, Birkin mentions Hermione in passing. They quarrel and Ursula throws the rings in the mud. While Birkin gazes at the gems' vivid colors against the mud, he realizes his error. Peace returns after some soothing words from him. They embrace and in the passion of their first intimacy, they spend the night in the country. Lawrence again uses repetition—here with 'dark', 'darkness', and 'loins of darkness'—to highlight pending gloom. (331)

In the next chapter, **Death and Love,** the darkness continues as the elder Mr. Crich dies slowly and with difficulty. Gerald's grief causes him to wander off one night. He walks adrift until he finds himself in front of Gudrun's house. Lawrence maintains the tone of "darkness and corrosive death" even as Gudrun accepts Gerald into her bed. Gerald sleeps quickly after their love-making but Gudrun remains awake, burdened not just by the weight of his body but by her thoughts. In **Marriage or Not,** Lawrence shifts back to the Ursula / Rupert dynamic. Birkin informs Gerald of his belief in the "*additional* perfect relationship between man and man—additional to marriage". (368) Gerald ". . . was strangely elated at Rupert's offer. Yet he was still more glad to reject it . . ." (368) The subject of marriage continues in the next chapter, **A Chair,** when Ursula and Birkin find a wooden arm-chair they like at an old market. When the two quarrel, Ursula gives away the chair to a young couple and accuses Rupert of bullying her, Hermione and Gerald. Birkin's only reply is that he seeks an "extra-human relationship" with Gerald. (379) When, in **Flitting,** Ursula announces at home that she will marry the following day her father reacts harshly and strikes her. Ursula storms out and seeks refuge at Birkin's home. They marry the next day. Later, Gerald tells Rupert he plans to take Gudrun away for the holidays. On learning this, Gudrun responds furiously at the thought that the two men exchange such confidences about her.

The four begin their holiday separately in the chapter **Gudrun in the Pompadour**. The trip does not augur well when, in London, Gerald and Gudrun stop at a club where they find Halliday, Pussum and the others already inebriated. Here Gudrun realizes that Gerald has had an affair with Pussum. When the others begin to ridicule the absent Birkin, Gudrun becomes furious and walks out. In **Continental**, the other couple begin their voyage under the ever present theme of "darkness". Only when they arrive at the chalet and Ursula sees her sister does she brighten. Birkin's depression worsens as the four discuss the future and England's place in it.

In the chapters **Snow** and **Snowed Up,** events at the hostel provoke tensions, create new triangles, and generally confirm the doom ahead. On their first outing to the snow-covered valley, Gudrun becomes so enraptured with the landscape that she does not hear Gerald when he declares his love. Later Gudrun senses a smothering feeling when Gerald is present. To intensify the growing separation, among the other guests at the hostel a young German named Loerke has caught her attention because of their mutual interest in art. A triangle of tension results. Then Ursula unexpectedly decides to leave. Without the other couple present, the conflict between Gudrun and Gerald escalates. The hostility peaks when they quarrel about the "little vermin" Loerke whom Gudrun plans to join in Dresden at his studio. Later, when Gerald sees Gudrun with the German guests, he thinks of killing her. Gudrun perceives danger from him but she laughs the fear away. In a ill-fated tobogganing outing, events turn violent when Gerald attacks Loerke and Gudrun. Realizing that taking her life has no value, Gerald instead feels an intense draining of all his strength, both physical and emotional. He walks toward a snowy ridge. "But he wandered on unconsciously, till he slipped and fell down, and as he fell something broke in his soul, and immediately he went to sleep." (494)

Finally in **Exeunt,** Gudrun remains detached in the face of Gerald's death. She sends a telegram to Ursula and Rupert and then coldly recounts the confrontation with Loerke. After seeing Gerald's dead body, Birkin tells Ursula that "he should have loved me . . ."(500) They return to England to bury Gerald. Gudrun goes to Dresden without further comment. Some time later, Rupert confesses to Ursula: "Having you, I can live all my life without anybody else, any other sheer intimacy. But to make it complete, really happy, I wanted eternal union with a man too: another kind of love . . . You can't have it, because it's false, impossible, she said. I don't believe that, he answered." (502) ❈

List of Characters in
Women in Love

Gerald Crich: Strong and domineering, Gerald enjoys managing the family mines and the power this affords him. He is proud of the scientifically based improvements he has made to the mines. Gerald exhibits physical prowess on many occasions as well as tendencies to dominate those around him. Gerald is attracted to Gudrun physically first and later emotionally but also pays attention to Birkin's compelling offer of a special friendship.

Gudrun Brangwen: Gudrun is a woman of creative talents whose interest in herself over others is expressed in her aversion to childbearing and her dislike for all things domestic. Gudrun shares confidences with her sister Ursula but does not always reveal her more private thoughts. She is both attracted and repulsed by Gerald's prowess and domineering ways and tires of their physical union shortly after it begins. In contrast, Gudrun responds to the sexually undemanding Loerke with whom she can discuss the finer themes of art.

Rupert Birkin: Caught up by his beliefs in society's decline and the need for a mystical communion between men and women, Rupert believes just as much in a lasting union with one woman as he does in a spiritual relationship with a man. Birkin openly expresses a love for Gerald Crich allowing Lawrence to develop and explore three separate couples in the text. He regularly rants about hypocrisy, quarrels when Hermione tries to take him on in philosophical debate, and eventually accepts Ursula's more mundane demands for romantic love.

Ursula Brangwen: A young and beautiful teacher at the local school, Ursula is bored by her life and surroundings. Her interest in Rupert becomes more intense and passionate in the face of her rivalry with Hermione. Ursula frequently dismisses Birkin's more philosophical views on love and life. Despite their frequent quarrels, Ursula believes marriage to Birkin is her only option in life.

Hermione Roddice: A tiresome and opinionated woman, Hermione considers herself inspired in everything she does and says. Hermione believes that only she truly understands Rupert and his needs. She makes endless attempts to undermine Ursula.

Loerke: This young German artist is a guest at the hostel in the Alps where Gerald and Gudrun stay. He is strangely attacked to Gudrun, shares his interest in art with her and provokes Gerald's jealousy. The tension from this triangle has tragic repercussions.

Mr. Crich: The head of the Crich family was loved by his miners for his charitable ways. Mr. Crich suffered though from his wife's long years of destructive behavior. He comes to depend greatly on Gerald and favors his youngest daughter, Winifred.

Winifred Crich: The youngest Crich child, she is bright, speaks French and German, and is interested in painting. Winifred welcomes Gudrun as her art teacher and new friend.

The Pussum: This socialite who pronounces her r's as w's catches Gerald's attention at a London club. Though made pregnant by another man, Miss Darrington seduces Gerald and uses him to further her plans in life.

Critical Views on
Women in Love

Letter from D. H. Lawrence to J. B. Pinker

[Two years after Lawrence wrote to Lady Ottoline about another suit, he recounts here that she is taking legal action against him for purportedly making Lady Ottoline the model for the unsympathetic character of Hermione in *Women in Love,* a thought that Lawrence finds preposterous.]

*To J. B. Pinker, from Higher Tregerthen, Cornwall,
20 February 1917*

My dear Pinker: Really, the world has gone completely dotty! Hermione is not much more like Ottoline Morrell than Queen Victoria, the house they claim as theirs is a Georgian house in Derbyshire I know very well—etc. Ottoline flatters herself. There *is* a hint of her in the character of Hermione: but so there is a hint of a million women, if it comes to that.

Anyway, they could make libel cases for ever, they haven't half a leg to stand on.

But it doesn't matter. It is no use trying to publish the novel in England in this state of affairs. There must come a change first. So it can all lie by. The world is mad, and has got a violent rabies that makes it turn on anything true, with frenzy. The novel can lie by till there is an end of the war and a change of feeling over the world. And poor vindictive old Ottoline can be left to her vanity of identifying herself with Hermione. What does it all matter!

—D. H. Lawrence, "Letter to J. B. Pinker." In *The Collected Letters of D. H. Lawrence,* Volume 1, ed. Henry T. Moore (New York: Viking, 1962): p. 502.

Gerald Doherty on Death and the Rhetoric of Representation

[Professor Doherty teaches literature at the University of Turku in Finland. He has published numerous articles on D. H. Lawrence as well as Joyce, Forster, and Woolf. In this study, Professor Doherty examines the representation of death in narrative fiction. The excerpt explains how Gerald faces his father's death and how Gerald's own death is described.]

Gerald's confrontation with his dying father provides the model for a "*flat Death*"—a "visible and audible" demise that, in its voiding of symbolic import, overwhelms him. Death's manifestation as a fleshly paroxysm, a painful physical seizure which nothing alleviates, intensifies the effect of pathos and horror. In their unredeemed corporeality, Mr. Crich's death-throes have a kind of convulsive carnality, a violent orgasmic intensity that brooks no turning away: no metaphoric gesture of transcendence can raise *them* up into significance. "Transfixed in horror," Gerald watches his father's last "frenzy of inhuman struggling," hears the "horrible, choking rattle," contemplates the "dark blood and mess pumping over the face of the agonized being." The vehemence of this description—its melodramatic insistence—conceals a radical absence of meaning: the reduction of death to a sequence of extreme physical sensations, to the agglomeration of the metonymic details that constitute it. As such the description also has sexual overtones: as a shattering climax to life, death appears as the body's last orgasmic seizure which, instead of restoring it and making it whole, disintegrates and destroys it.

Precisely because Gerald is unable to metaphorize death—to perceive it in terms of transfers and transformations—he is subsequently caught up in a chain of events that extends his father's death-drama by reproducing metonymic substitutes for it. Take, for example, his visit to the churchyard soon after his father's death. Through contiguous associations with the funereal and the macabre, this visit extends the death-drama, evoking through its detailed description the material and sensuous essence of death. As Gerald walks among the tombstones, he reacts with "revulsion" to the "heaped pallor of old white flowers . . . cold and clammy" to the touch, to the "raw scent of chrysanthemums and tube-roses," and to the "cold and sticky" clay of the graves. In carrying the clay on his boots into Gudrun's bedroom (where he makes his way immediately after the churchyard visit), Gerald literally carries mortality into his sexual encounter with Gudrun. By bringing eros and death into contiguous contact, he infects one with the other. As he pours "all his pent-up darkness and corrosive death" into her, she, a passive subject, receives him "as a vessel filled with his bitter potion of death." They trade death in a kind of metonymic exchange. Since this exchange lacks precisely the transformations associated with metaphoric transfers, it involves only the simple passing of an untransformed essence back and forth from one to the other. As a climax, Gudrun receives the "terrible frictional violence of death . . . in an ecstasy of subjection in throes of acute, violent sensation." Indeed Gudrun's orgasmic disintegration has its closest counterpart in Mr. Crich's deathly paroxysms: both are forms of a metonymic reduction and fragmentation that sunders, isolates and destroys.

The description of Gerald's own death, as he wanders away among the snow-slopes of the Alps, wavers between representing death as the preordained destiny toward which his own momentum compels him ("He wanted so to come to the end—he had had enough"), and as a purely contingent event, the outcome of the randomness of his movements, completely haphazard and out of control ("He drifted, as on a wind, veered and went drifting away"). Underscoring this tension, the text juxtaposes two antagonistic images at the climax of the death drama: the "half-buried crucifix, a little Christ under a little sloping hood, at the top of a pole"—*the* central Western symbol of metaphoric death, which is geared to sacrificial transcendence (and which functions as an index of what Gerald's end might have been)—and Gerald's fearful apprehension of his own death in terms of a sudden "murder," the irruption of a casual violence, which fills him with "dread." His momentary death is encoded metonymically in the same way as his father's; both are configured as the sudden snapping of the "knot" that tied the life-elements together, a dive into literal death: "as he fell something broke in his soul, and immediately he went to sleep."

The final episode ("Exeunt") extends the representation of death as a radical metonymy, resistant to metaphoric transfiguration, to its extreme limit. In these mortuary scenes, Gerald's corpse is displayed—untranslated, unsubsumed—in all its ugly abjection and pathos. It is fixed in its hideous "thereness," inhuman and sterile. A bleak contrast is established between the Birkin who remembers Gerald with commitment and love—"He should have loved me . . . I offered him"—and the Birkin who reacts with "disgust," appalled at the sight of "the inert body lying there . . . so coldly dead, a carcase." Deathly effects proliferate through contiguous association with the corpse that evokes them. Birkin's prolonged contemplation foregrounds the essential meaninglessness of the corpse—Gerald's "dead mass of maleness, repugnant," his body, "like clay, like bluish, corruptible ice," his "last terrible look of cold, mute Matter" (the substantive now capitalized to evoke Matter's resistance to transformation). While these cumulative details insist on the absolute closure of death, simultaneously they deprive it of an explanation. They suggest that no special meaning inheres in the death-event beyond the metonymic details that go to compose it. There is no going-beyond, no metaphoric transcendence to raise up the corpse into higher significance. Gerald's "inert mass" resists precisely those transfers and transformations for which Birkin's word "love" functions as catalyst. In Birkin's perception, "[t]hose who die, and dying still can love, still believe, do not die. They live still in the beloved." In rhetorical terms, only a metaphoric reaching out toward a transfiguration ensures a fresh revelation of meaning.

>—Gerald Doherty, "Death and the Rhetoric of Representation in D. H. Lawrence's *Women in Love*," *Mosaic* 27, no. 1 (Winnipeg, Man.: March 1994): pp. 63–65.

EARL INGERSOLL ON STAGING THE GAZE

> [Professor Ingersoll is the author of *D. H. Lawrence, Desire, and Narrative* (2001). Ingersoll maintains that the two couple structure of the novel enhances its impact. In the essay, he discusses how this structure is framed by references to eyes and seeing. The opening action of the novel begins when Gudrun decides to "look at" a wedding. In this excerpt, Ingersoll points to the maturing of the relationship

between Birkin and Ursula which is strengthened by gazes to a point of almost mystic vision.]

One aspect of the complex relationship between the two couples—Ursula Brangwen and Rupert Birkin, Gudrun Brangwen and Gerald Crich—is the pronounced contrast in the development of visual exchange between the characters. It might be noted at the outset that a concern with looking at and being looked at in Lawrence's work is not unique to *Women in Love*. In *The Rainbow*, for example, Tom Brangwen looks at Lydia Lensky passing him on the road and "involuntarily" blurts out, "That's her," and later the young Ursula begins to read her own beauty and desirability in the impassioned gaze of her future lover Anton Skrebensky. These more conventional expressions of visual exchange offer a good starting point since they persist in *Women in Love*. They are increasingly displaced, however, by more intricate expressions of looking.

The contrast between conventional and more complicated expressions of visual exchange is evident in *Women in Love* from the beginning in the descriptions of the two couples' developing relationships. Birkin first becomes significantly aware of Ursula during Hermione's theatricalizing of the Ruth story in her drawing room at Breadalby. What he sees is an Ursula who is "like a strange unconscious bud of powerful womanhood. He was unconsciously drawn to her. She was his future." Birkin's looking at Ursula here and recognizing in an instant that she represents "his future" repeats the healthier consequences of visual exchange in Tom's recognition of Lydia as his future wife. Unlike the Gudrun-Gerald relationship, the growing love of Ursula and Birkin is noticeably lacking in looking and being looked at, with one notable exception. The exception occurs in the "Moony" chapter in which Ursula comes upon Birkin stoning the moon's reflection. Before she is aware of his presence, however, Ursula suddenly senses the moon "watching her," and we are told that "she suffered being exposed to it." Her reaction against the moon's reflection on Willey Water seems to generate the presence of another watcher, whom she immediately knows must be Birkin. Because for a long time she does not betray her presence as a watcher, Ursula becomes a voyeur. Why else is she uncomfortable that he might do "something he would not wish to be seen doing"? When he becomes aware of her presence while he stones the moon's reflection upon the water, it is clear that his intent gaze upon the moon's reflection has been "reading," or calling up in his unconscious, an aversion that mutely speaks to Ursula's aversion to this light and her unspoken desire for a darkness beyond the darkness of the night.

The promise of that other darkness is offered in the lovemaking in the "Excurse" chapter. In the parlor where they have had their tea, Ursula and Birkin make love, in a fashion. Visual exchange becomes prominent in the scene, yet it is implicated in a renewal of vision. Here the visual exchange seems to highlight mutuality and a depth of tenderness released by the power of the metaphoric:

> She *looked* at him . . . New eyes were opened in her soul, she *saw* a strange creature from another world, in him . . . She recalled again the old magic of the Book of Genesis, where the Sons of God *saw* the daughters of men, that they were fair. And he was one of these, one of these strange creatures from the beyond, *looking* down at her, and *seeing* she was fair.

This scene functions as the *annunciation* of the potential in their relationship. That potential moves toward its realization in their night of love in Sherwood Forest. Looking at and being looked at are utterly erased as possibilities in "pure night." Only darkness and silence reign in this kingdom of tenderness and touch, "never to be seen with the eye."

In these key scenes of Ursula and Birkin's maturing love, visual factors contribute to an enhancement of something approaching the traditional mystic vision. It is the vision of love for which Lawrence borrowed the scriptural language of "a new heaven and a new earth." It is not a looking at, but a way of seeing the world anew, with eyes able to "see" at last. Even then, this seeing is subordinate to the darkness of the "body of mysterious night," just as "silence" is privileged over even the most inspired "speech." These expressions of a more "positive" visual exchange are crucial to the narrative's attempt at balancing interest in the two couples. In their own frequently underacknowledged way, they function as a counterpart to a powerful variant that might be called a perversion of looking. ⟨. . .⟩

Returning to *Women in Love,* we discover the dominance of looking and being looked at from the very beginning. The opening scene ends with the suggestion of Gudrun, the incipient watcher in this text, that they go for a walk: "Shall we go out and *look at* that wedding?" (emphasis added). The walk to the church becomes painful to Gudrun, "exposed to every stare," of these "uneasy, watchful common people." At the same time, of course, she invites their stares with her brightly-colored stockings. Her surprisingly violent reaction to one spectator's comment prepares us for her attraction to Gerald:

> "A sudden fierce anger swept over the girl, violent and murderous. She would have liked them all to be annihilated, cleared away, so that the world was left clear for her. How she hated walking up the churchyard path . . . *in their sight*" (emphasis added).

Her revulsion against being looked at by these ghoulish spectators is so great that she almost misses the opportunity to be a spectator herself at the Crich wedding, the first of several close encounters with Gerald Crich.

The wedding party and its spectators provide Gudrun with a diverting spectacle at first. However, it is Gerald upon whom her gaze "lights," perhaps because he has "the strange, guarded look, the unconscious glisten," which becomes the signature of his personality. The statement that she "lighted on him at once" suggests a linkage of staring or gazing with an aggressive, almost predatory assault upon Gerald. In a striking inversion of Tom's instantaneous recognition of Lydia, Gudrun says, "That's *him*!" so to speak, an ominous indication of her future role as active pursuer/watcher of Gerald. "I shall know more of that man," she says, emphasizing that seeing is at least a double phenomenon here, for gazing at/familiarizing herself with Gerald will be her way of knowing him. In this way, she will "know" Gerald in a mode traditionally reserved for the male eye for which the love object to be pursued is a complex of surfaces in which the eye becomes ensnared.

Here, however, Gudrun becomes involved in the gaze by training her eyes upon Gerald as an object of desire. Clearly the gaze is "reading" her voyeurism, implicit in her aversion to being looked at, an aversion which the narrative has foregrounded in her revulsion against being stared at by the "watchful common people" on the way to the church. She stares at Gerald as though he has mesmerized, or "magnetised" her. What the gaze is reading in her is Gudrun's "violent and murderous" impulses, suggested by her recognition of similar impulses in him: "His totem is the wolf." Gerald's "clear northern flesh and his fair hair" are metaphorized as "cold sunshine refracted through crystals of ice." In this way, Gerald's "god" is Apollo, the Greek god of light, order, and knowing through the eye, the same Apollo, whose totem was also the wolf. Gerald is a variety of the earliest graphic evidence of classical Greek civilization—the kouros, or "Apollo," the "beautiful boy," to use Camille Paglia's term, the first sex object of Western desire.

Gudrun's bizarre reaction to knowing Gerald visually, that reaction frequently viewed as "orgasmic," suggests the power of the gaze in reading the unconscious in her. As she stares at Gerald, who seems at this point not yet aware of the role chosen for him as love object/exhibitionist in this theater of the gaze, Gudrun is being read as an active, even aggressive, and potentially sadistic watcher:

> She was tortured with desire to *see* him again, a nostalgia, a necessity to *see* him again, to *make sure* it was not all a mistake, that she was not deluding herself, that she really felt this strange and overwhelming sensation on his account, this knowledge of him in her essence, this powerful *apprehension* of him.

If her reaction seems "orgasmic," it is the result of the abruptness of her "lighting" upon Gerald as her potentially perverse soul-mate in this dramatization of the "instincts and their vicissitudes." It might be noted also that *her* visual knowledge of *him* is an "apprehension," i.e., at one and the same time, a "perception," a "conception," an "arrest," and a "foreboding."

In a sense, we are witnessing in this scene the first stage of the instinct of voyeurism and its vicissitude of exhibitionism. Gudrun, in her aversion to being looked at, has discovered, as though for the first time, the power of watching, the knowledge and control which come through the eye. Perhaps because Gudrun understands her "femininity" as a function of her being a vulnerable, powerless object of male staring and rejects it, she adopts the traditionally "male" position in the staging of this instinct and its reversal. If her "orgasmic" experience of knowing Gerald through the eye—that "paroxysm of violent sensation"—is erotically organized, then it functions as a fitting annunciation of what has seemed for readers of the novel a sadomasochistic relationship that reverses conventional gender identities. From this annunciation scene on, she will come to enjoy the power of controlling/humiliating the increasingly masochistic Gerald.

—Earl Ingersoll, "Staging the Gaze in D. H. Lawrence's *Women in Love*," *Studies in the Novel* 26 (Fall 1994): pp. 269–270, 273–275.

※

Eric P. Levy on Lawrence's Psychology of Void and Center

[Professor Levy is the author of *Beckett and the Voice of Species: A Study of the Prose Fiction* (1980) as well as many articles on Shakespeare's *Hamlet* and Virginia Woolf. This study looks at centered and void characters and the type of love each character represents. In this excerpt, Professor Levy focuses on Gerald and Gudrun whom he considers void characters whose inner emptiness prevents them from experiencing complete love.]

Rapture and despair: communion and isolation—these are the contraries connected with the peaks. They are also the contraries connected with love throughout the novel. Birkin and Ursula have their own way of transcending this destructive dialectic. Yet the love between Gerald and Gudrun is inescapably controlled by it. For each of them, the ultimate purpose of love is to transfer to the other the sense of rejection and exclusion that exposure to love can bring, just as it did in childhood. At bottom, as void characters, both Gudrun and Gerald can conceive of love only from the perspective of the child whom love bullied or deprived. From that child's perspective, the adult or source of love is exactly like the bronze horse: hard, cold, and impervious to pity for the child's vulnerability. Significantly, Gerald is as much connected with the little girl on the horse as Gudrun is; for, in an earlier chapter ("Breadalby"), Birkin reacts to Gerald's legs in a way that clearly suggests those of the girl on the horse: "Yet they moved Birkin with a sort of pathos, tenderness, as if they were childish." In the description of Loerke's statuette, the legs of the "tender" girl dangle "childishly" and "pathetically."

Such vulnerability can never feel secure with love—even though protective love is its greatest need. The peaks represent the invulnerability wished by that insecurity. Both Gudrun and Gerald turn their love into a deadly *agon* or "contest" whose goal is to translate the victor to that "unapproachable" summit where his weakness can never be threatened. Gerald moves literally in this direction as he hikes to death toward "the top of the mountain." But Gudrun's ascent is just as vivid—if not as literal: "But it was a fight to the death.... One slip, and she was lost. She had a strange, tense, exhilarated sickness in her body, as one who is in peril of falling from a great height, but who does not look down, does not admit the fear." In effect, Gudrun climbs over Gerald to reach her peak. More precisely, she converts Gerald's enraged response to rejection into proof of her own invincibility.

In Lawrence's psychology, no experience but death is more transforming than falling in love. Centered characters like Ursula and Birkin can accept this process: "It was a fight to the death between them—or to new life: though in what the conflict lay, no one could say." But void characters like Gerald and Gudrun cannot respond to love in the same way. They are far too threatened by their own inner emptiness ever to trust an experience that will overwhelm their sense of identity altogether. At bottom, love for them resolves into fear and anger: fear of absorption or complete rejection by another and anger at such an outrage.

—Eric P. Levy, "Lawrence's Psychology of Void and Center in *Women in Love*," *The D. H. Lawrence Review* 23, no. 1 (Delaware: University of Delaware Press, Spring 1991): pp. 15–16.

NORMAN MAILER ON THE PRISONER OF SEX

[As controversial and provocative as the artist he describes here, Norman Mailer takes on Kate Millet's feminist criticism of Lawrence and offers his own opinions on the artist in the chapter entitled "The Advocate." In this excerpt, Mailer comments on the relationship between Birkin and

Gerald in *Women in Love* as corresponding to Lawrence's own 'temptation' with homosexuality, his decline in health and the repercussions on his sexual interests that occur between the writing of this novel and *Lady Chatterley's Lover*.]

These are the years when he flirts with homosexuality, but is secretly, we may assume, obsessed with it. For he is still in need of that restorative sex he can no longer find, and since his psyche was originally shaped to be homosexual, homosexuality could yet be his peace. Except it could not, not likely, for his mind could hardly give up the lust to dominate. Homosexuality becomes a double irony—he must now seek to dominate men physically more powerful than himself. The paradoxes of this position result in the book *Aaron's Rod* which is about a male love affair (which never quite takes place) between a big man and a little man. The little man does the housework, plays nursemaid to the big man when he is ill, and ends by dominating him, enough to offer the last speech in the book.

> All men say, they want a leader. Then let them in their souls submit to some greater soul than theirs . . . You, Aaron, you too have the need to submit. You, too, have the need livingly to yield to a more heroic soul, to give yourself. You know you have [but] . . . perhaps you'd rather die than yield. And so, die you must. It is your affair.

He has separated the theme from himself and reversed the roles, but he will die rather than yield, even though earlier in the book he was ready to demonstrate that platonic homosexuality saves. It is the clear suggestion that Aaron recovers only because Lilly anoints his naked body, lays on hands after doctors and medicines had failed.

> Quickly he uncovered the blond lower body of his patient, and began to rub the abdomen with oil, using a slow, rhythmic, circulating motion, a sort of massage. For a long time he rubbed finely and steadily, then went over the whole of the lower body, mindless, as if in a sort of incantation. He rubbed every speck of the man's lower body—the abdomen, the buttocks, the thighs and knees, down to his feet, rubbed it all warm and glowing with camphorated oil, every bit of it, chafing the toes swiftly, till he was almost exhausted. Then Aaron was covered up again, and Lilly sat down in fatigue to look at his patient.

> He saw a change. The spark had come back into the sick eyes, and the faint trace of a smile, faintly luminous, into the face. Aaron was regaining himself. But Lilly said nothing. He watched his patient fall into a proper sleep.

Another of his heroes, Birkin, weeps in strangled tones before the coffin of Gerald. It is an earlier period in Lawrence's years of homosexual temptation; the pain is sharper, the passion is stronger. "He should have loved me," he said. "I offered him." And his wife is repelled, "recoiled aghast from him as he sat . . . making a strange, horrible sound of tears." They are the sickly sounds of a man who feels ready to die in some part of himself because the other man would never yield.

But homosexuality would have been the abdication of Lawrence as a philosopher-king. Conceive how he must have struggled against it! In all those middle years he moves slowly from the man who is sickened because the other did not yield, to the man who will die because he, himself, will not yield. But he is bitter, and with a rage which could burn half the world. It is burning his lungs.

Then it is too late. He is into his last years. He is into the five last years of his dying. He has been a victim of love, and will die for lack of the full depth of a woman's love for him—what a near to infinite love he had needed. So he has never gotten to that place where he could deliver himself to the unknown, be "without reserves or defenses . . . cast off everything . . . and cease to be, so that that which is perfectly ourselves can take place in us," no, he was never able to go that far. By the time he began *Lady Chatterley*, he must have known the fight was done; he had never been able to break out of the trap of his lungs, nor out of the cage of his fashioning. He had burned too many holes in too many organs trying to reach into more manhood than the course of his nerves could carry, he was done; but he was a lover, he wrote *Lady Chatterley*, he forgave, he wrote his way a little further toward death, and sang of the wonders of creation and the glory of men and women in the rut and lovely of a loving fuck.

> "When a woman gets absolutely possessed by her own will, her own will set against everything, then it's fearful, and she should be shot at last."
> "And shouldn't men be shot at last, if they get possessed by their own will?"
> "Ay!—the same!"

The remark is muttered, the gamekeeper rushes on immediately to talk of other matters, but it has been made, Lawrence has closed the circle, the man and the woman are joined, separate and joined.

—Norman Mailer, *The Prisoner of Sex* (Boston: Little, Brown and Company, 1971): pp. 157–160.

DAVID PARKER ON THE IDEOLOGICAL UNKNOWN

[Author of *Ethics Theory and the Novel* (1994), David Parker takes recent poststructuralist theory as his point of departure in this essay where he argues against suppressing the canon in favor of Marxist historical or psychological perspectives. Instead, Parker looks at what he calls the 'dynamic interrelatedness' of the ideology of 'innocence versus social being' and concepts of good and evil. To do this, he contrasts the characters of the two women, Ursula and Gudrun, and the two men, Rupert and Gerald.]

Most accounts of *Women in Love,* such as the one in Dan Jacobson's recent book ("*Women in Love* and the Death of the Will" in *Adult Pleasures,* London, 1988), stress the polarization between two sets of characters, one struggling through to freedom and life, the other going down the slope, with the rest of the race, to various forms of death. This view of the novel has of course a lot to be said for it. The opening dialogue, for instance, immediately presents a distinction between two ways of thinking about something—which turn out to be, more importantly, two ways of being.

On the one hand, there is Ursula, "calm and considerate", deciding that she doesn't know whether she *really wants* to get married; for her, it will depend on what sort of man turns up, which can't be known in advance. Her calm already hints at a fundamental trust, or underlying ease, in face of this unknown future. The prose is soon to suggest the shaping underlife from which these thoughts and words come. Though she feels curiously "suspended", we're told, Ursula accedes to what she senses darkly at centre: a new potential life like an infant in the womb, held in by "integuments" but pressing for birth. Leaving aside for the moment the ideological question of the sort of transformation—narrative this image might seem to imply, it's clear after a few pages that Ursula's capacity to be at ease with uncertainty is connected with a strong potentiality for growth. In this first page, her "I don't know" and "I'm not sure" are the first hints of that, and it's important to note that they indicate an openness, not least of *mind*.

Gudrun by contrast wants to be "quite definite"; for her it seems possible that "in the abstract" one might need the *experience* of having been married. The dramatic imagining also suggests that, despite this drive for definiteness, Gudrun isn't, as Ursula is, really "considering" possible consequences of marrying for the experience. When Ursula points to the most likely consequence, that it will be the end of experience, Gudrun "attends" to the question as if for the first time. Two things then happen; the conversation comes temporarily "to a close", and Gudrun, almost angrily, rubs out part of her drawing in a way that indicates suppressed emotion. These little closures keep occurring, and always they're brought about by Gudrun. A bit later, Ursula questions her about her magnificently stated motive for coming back home—"*reculer pour mieux sauter*":

> "But where can one jump *to*?"
> "Oh, it doesn't matter," said Gudrun, somewhat superbly. "If one jumps over the edge, one is bound to land somewhere."
> "But isn't it very risky?" asked Ursula.
> A slow, mocking smile dawned on Gudrun's face.
> "Ah!" she said, laughing. "What is it all but words!"
> And so again she closed the conversation. But Ursula was still brooding.
> "And how do you find home, now you have come back to it?" she asked.
> Gudrun paused for some moments, coldly, before answering. Then, in a cold, truthful voice, she said:
> "I find myself completely out of it."
> "And father?"
> Gudrun looked at Ursula, almost with resentment, as if brought to bay.
> "I haven't thought about him: I've refrained," she said coldly.
> "Yes," wavered Ursula; and the conversation was really at an end. The sisters found themselves confronted by a void, a terrifying chasm, as if they had looked over the edge.

> They worked on in silence for some time. Gudrun's cheek was flushed with repressed emotion. She resented its having been called into being.

Gudrun's conversational closures show a way of talking and thinking—or rather, *not*-thinking—that's at least as interested in the impression it's making on others as it is in getting at the truth of something. As the fashionable cynicism of "What is it all but words!" reminds us, this is the sociolect of glittering Chelsea bohemia. It is what poststructuralism would call a "discourse": the cynical "words" to some extent speak Gudrun. It's a discourse, above all, of power, which is exercised precisely in clipping off whatever subject might reveal one, give one away, show a chink in the armour. The chilly formality of "I've refrained" does this to Ursula, who until then wants to go on thinking about the matter of father, to think it through, not least for her own sake. Like everything else, the words add to Gudrun's impressiveness, but they also instantly resist any possibility either of closer contact with Ursula or, more significantly, of getting at the blocked feelings that are obviously calling out for expression within herself. For Lawrence's imagining insists that the expressed "words" of any individual or group, their sociolect or discourse, can't really be understood as such without reference to the whole state of being they involve. Gudrun in a sense *is* in a prison house of language ("what is it *all* but words"), but that's only intelligible in terms of the underlying "repressed emotion" her particular language both manifests and helps to contain. It's a language of repression, of resistance, in other words, designed, like her stockings, to cover up magnificently. And already, the novel is suggesting the price to be paid for this magnificence—thwarted energy, the feeling of everything withering in the bud. ⟨ . . . ⟩

Right from the beginning, Birkin has been saying other characters' lines in a way that reveals the repressed "social being" in him. One extremely telling moment is at the wedding at Shortlands when Mrs Crich hints that she'd like him to be Gerald's friend:

> Birkin looked down into her eyes, which were blue, and watching heavily. He could not understand them. "Am I my brother's keeper?" he said to himself, almost flippantly.
> Then he remembered with a slight shock, that that was Cain's cry. And Gerald was Cain, if anybody. Not that he was Cain, either, although he had slain his brother. There

was such a thing as pure accident. . . . Or is this not true, is there no such thing as pure accident? Has *everything* that happens a universal significance? Has it? Birkin pondering as he stood there, had forgotten Mrs Crich, as she had forgotten him.

He did not believe that there was any such thing as accident. It all hung together, in the deepest sense.

Assuming that Birkin is right and there's no such thing as pure accident, then what are we to make of Birkin "accidentally" uttering Cain's cry, and then when he remembers whose cry it is instantly associating it with Gerald? What it all suggests is something that Freud, who didn't believe in accidents either, would have seen as a significant slip, a revelation "in the deepest sense" of an aspect of Birkin that he didn't want to know about—namely the Cain in himself. One way in which Birkin is Cain isn't hard to see; after all, he is a mass brother-murderer in his often-expressed wish that the rest of mankind would simply disappear. He has just said so to Mrs Crich:

"Not many people amount to anything at all," he answered, forced to go much deeper than he wanted to. "They jingle and giggle. It would be much better if they were just wiped out. Essentially, they don't exist, they aren't there."

Saying this kind of thing is obviously much more disturbing to Birkin than he can allow himself to know, which is one reason for resisting Dan Jacobson's assertion that Birkin is allowed by the novel to get away with this sort of sentiment "without being accused by the narrative voice or the other characters of manifesting a murderously diseased will." What this overlooks is a much more subtle form of placing: Birkin's annihilating wishes and Gerald's brother-killing as a ruthless mineowner—thus annihilating his father's sort of troubled brotherhood—are being unmistakably linked.

In this and in other ways Birkin and Gerald are seen to be brothers in spirit if not in blood long before explicit *Blutbruderschaft* comes into question. As with the sisterhood of Ursula and Gudrun, this is so even when the imagining of them draws strong attention to difference. The dialogue that concludes "Shortlands" for instance has Birkin analysing Gerald's conventionality and opposing it to true spontaneity, when suddenly the focus shifts to what connects them:

> There was a pause of strange enmity between the two men, that was very near to love. It was always the same between them; always their talk brought them into a deadly nearness of contact, a strange, perilous intimacy which was either hate or love, or both. They parted with apparent inconcern, as if their going apart were a trivial occurrence. And they really kept it to the level of trivial occurrence. Yet the heart of each burned from the other. They burned with each other, inwardly. This they would never admit. They intended to keep their relationship a casual free-and-easy friendship, they were not going to be so unmanly and unnatural as to allow any heart-burning between them. They had not the faintest belief in deep relationship between man and man, and their disbelief prevented any development of their powerful but suppressed friendliness.

Here it is *Birkin,* as much as Gerald, who's showing that, as Birkin himself has just said, "It's the hardest thing in the world to act spontaneously on one's impulses...." This is only remarkable because in context it was a dictum directed at *Gerald's* supposedly Cain-like suppressed desire/fear of having his gizzard slit. What Birkin's whole argument suppresses in fact is his own suppressed feeling for Gerald, which has a good deal to do with why it *is* such a provocatively cutting sort of argument. In yet another Cain-like way then, Birkin is denying that in himself which is common to both men; and he has the analytical knife out for Gerald precisely because, at some level, that brotherhood itself is deeply "perilous" to him.

> —David Parker, "Into the Ideological Unknown," *The Critical Review,* no. 30 (The Australian National University, Canberra, 1990): pp. 137–140.

John Worthen on the First Version of *Women in Love*

[Professor of D. H. Lawrence Studies at the University of Nottingham, John Worthen is the author of *D. H. Lawrence: A Literary Life* (1989) and *D. H. Lawrence: The Early Years 1885–1912* (1991). Having edited several of Lawrence's texts for Cambridge University Press, Professor Worthen shares his findings in this essay on the first version of *Women in Love*. In the following excerpt, he presents the differences in Ursula's characterization in the text from 1916 and the 1921 novel.]

Ursula, too, is a good deal more rebellious (and less confident) than she would be in 1921. Although she agrees to go away with Birkin, into what he confidently assures her is his own world, her reservations about spending all her time there take on the quality of ironical criticisms of the idea: "I may go to London sometimes to the music-hall, mayn't I? I love it so." Birkin can only grumble at her: "It bores me. But you do as you like." When it comes to sending in their resignations, it is Ursula who brings them to the point of doing so (in the 1921 novel the decision is mutual); and it is she who objects to the idea of people suspecting the simultaneity of their resigning. In 1921, she will say "I don't care . . . it doesn't matter, does it?" In 1916 she is much more determined, compared with Birkin's casualness: "Isn't it rather horrid, if everybody knows . . . I feel I don't want them to. It isn't their affair."

Above all, they do not leave the room to go and make love climactically in Sherwood Forest, as in 1921. They have the same exchange—"Shall we go?" "As you like"—but what follows is one of Birkin's most revealingly honest moments. He finds himself wanting Ursula sexually, whilst simultaneously desiring *not* to want her.

> It was not this, not this he wanted with her—not the poignant ecstasies of sex passion. Yet he did want them also, with an old craving of habit. And the desire seemed like death to him. For beyond this was the small, yearning hope of a new sort of love, a new sort of intercourse, that was gentle and still and so happy, it was chastity and innocence of itself. This, this new, gentle possession, should be the true consummation of their marriage.

He is thus as theoretical—or hypothetical—about sex as he is elsewhere about relationship in general: it is he who has the *ideas* about what their relationship could be like, what its "true consummation" should be. He is looking for something which—whilst sexual—is also not going to be as violent as "the old, fierce, destroying embrace"; he fears that sex of the old kind (at least, of the old kind which *he* has experienced) will destroy relationship. He tells Ursula about his fears—and the last three pages of the chapter concentrate on this subject almost exclusively.

Ursula is both fascinated and annoyed: "She had not been prepared for this. She felt as if he accused her, accused her of some harlotry." She, after all, shares none of his fears, nor does she participate in his rebellion against the past. Rather sensibly, she suggests that "one can't decide these things in this fashion. . . . One can't be so deliberate. It is indecent. We must take what comes." Her slightly indignant insouciance is however met by Birkin's customary stonewalling. He insists that "one chooses. At length, one must choose. I know one must."

All the time, however, he is hoping against hope that she will ignore his theories and just give herself to him, so that he can indulge in passion without blaming himself (presumably blaming her instead). But he ends up rather helplessly telling her that he has had that kind of sex and is finished with it; or, to be exact, "whether I have finished with it—heaven help us, I don't know—." This leaves her in the same state as it leaves him: "'And I don't know,' she murmured, helplessly."

> At last he made a move to her.
> "At any rate," he said, looking down at her and touching her cheek with the tips of his fingers. "I know I love you—I love your face." The knowledge was a great comfort to him, a rock. "And if we go wrong—I shall know—ich habe es nicht gewollt. . . . "

Knowing that he loves her—at least, that he loves her face—is a very odd kind of "rock" on which to found a belief; the contrast between the softness of the face (and the touch), and the hardness of the rock, suggests how much Birkin is trying to convince himself. He also gives himself (in the Kaiser's "I did not want it") the excuse for possible failure with Ursula which—in the 1921 novel—is linked with his failure with Gerald Crich. Such things make Birkin's certainty about his love intensely ambiguous. ⟨...⟩

Gerald's final walk to his death is nearly identical in the two texts. But the end of the novel, in the next chapter, shows one of the fundamental differences between 1916 and 1921. For one thing, Birkin's reaction to Gudrun is very different; he is "full of judgement," and she is conscious that he judges her; his manner is "damning," altered to "abstracted" in 1921. But this is linked with Birkin's utterly different series of responses to dead Gerald. Birkin's grief

> was chiefly misery. He could not bear that the beautiful, virile Gerald was a heap of inert matter, a transient heap, rubbish on the face of the earth, really.

His reflections on Gerald would, in the 1921 text, turn into a strange kind of consolation; he would develop his ideas of "the mystery of creation" as "fathomless, infallible, inexhaustible," and he would find them a profound comfort. In 1916, just the opposite happens. Birkin is frozen too: dead like Gerald.

> And still Birkin's heart was frozen in his breast. This, then, was the end. He had loved Gerald, he loved him still. But the love was frozen in his breast, frozen by the death that possessed himself, as well as Gerald.

There are no consoling thoughts about creation or the creative mystery. Only when Birkin breaks down into tears do the 1916 and 1921 texts briefly come close again. But developments swiftly follow in 1921—Birkin's insistence to Ursula that he has loved Gerald, Ursula's complaint "You've got me," and the ending of the novel concentrating entirely on the relationship between Birkin and Ursula. It ends, of course, with them both back in England, talking about "two kinds of love," and (as always) disagreeing, down to the famous last line: "'I don't believe that,' he answered."

None of this had happened in 1916. Birkin's tears of grief over Gerald horrify Ursula and she slips wordlessly out of the room at the bottom of the novel's penultimate page—and thus out of the novel for good. It is not with the relationship of Birkin and Ursula that this text will end. There remains a single, strange, deeply moving final page of Birkin's mourning for Gerald, containing some of Lawrence's most emotional writing. It is not just grief for dead

Gerald: "It was not the death he could not bear, but the nothingness of the life and the death put together. It killed the quick of one's life." And the novel ends like this:

> He could not bear it. His heart seemed to be torn in his chest.
> "But even then," he strove to say, "we needn't all be like that. All is not lost, because many are lost.—I am not afraid or ashamed to die and be dead."

Against the grain, Birkin thus stresses what he barely believes: that all is not lost, in spite of the many who are lost. He is oddly like Milton's Satan, insisting against overwhelming odds that "All is not lost...." But what he feels is death.

In 1917, of course, this could only have been read as a direct reference to the war, and to its dreadful losses, with Birkin attempting to stand clear and see differently. But the novel was by now beyond all hope of being published, partly because of the final context in which the novel can be set: perhaps the most significant of all. The 1916 First *"Women in Love"* is a war novel to a much greater extent than the 1921 text; in part because one reads it differently, as the work of 1916, and in part because some passages which were subsequently cut, or changed, bore very heavily on the world of 1916–17 and would have struck 1917 readers with particular force.

> —John Worthen, "The First '*Women in Love*,'" *The D. H. Lawrence Review* 28, no. 1–2, (Delaware: University of Delaware Press, 1998): pp. 12–13, 18–20.

Plot Summary of
Lady Chatterley's Lover

(Quotations from the text are from Lawrence, D. H. *Lady Chatterley's Lover*. Michael Squires, ed. London: Penguin, 1994.)

Critics have paid much attention to the three versions of *Lady Chatterley's Lover,* in particular to the evolution of Constance's character, her state of isolation in an obviously doomed marriage, and the denouement of her relationship with the gamekeeper Oliver Mellors, called Parkin in the first two versions. The chronology of the three versions spans the years 1926 through early 1928 when Lawrence finishes the third and final version. The action of the text can be divided into three parts—all with Constance as a focus: in the first part (chapters 1–7), the very bleak life of Constance at the side of her paralyzed husband centers on her tedious activities and her ever growing desires to "get away to the wood". The second part (chapters 8–14) concerns Constance's rebirth as a consequence of her passionate relationship with and subsequent love for Mellors, the estate gamekeeper. In the final section (chapters 15–19), escape from Wragby becomes a complicated reality for Constance.

In **Chapter One,** Lawrence explains that when his older brother Herbert is killed, Clifford becomes the family heir. Constance comes from a family in the intelligentsia and spends her youth in close company with her sister Hilda receiving a more "unconventional upbringing" (6) than most. By the time they were eighteen both girls had had their first affairs and considered the sexual aspect of love as being less spectacular than advertised. Constance was a friend of Clifford's before the time of his brother's death. Sir Geoffrey, Clifford's father, emphasized Clifford's responsibility to produce an heir. So Constance and Clifford married and spent a month's honeymoon before Clifford joined the war where Clifford was wounded, leaving him paralyzed from the waist down: **Chapter Two** begins as the two return to Wragby Hall to begin newly married life. Lady Chatterley is somewhat shocked at "the utter soulless ugliness of the coal-and-iron Midlands" (13) where the family home faces the coal pits in Tevershall, the nearby village. Because of his injury, Clifford avoids anyone other than Constance and the servants. He sits in a wheel chair, remote and detached. "Yet he was absolutely dependent on her—he needed her every moment." (16) Nevertheless, Clifford is ambitious and determined to augment his estate income by writing. In the second year of their marriage, when Sir Malcolm, Constance's father, visits, he confronts the couple separately but with the same warning—Clifford should not let circumstances turn Constance into a "demi-vierge". Constance's restlessness grows in **Chapter Three.** Her constant desire is to "get away to the wood". Here Lawrence begins what he develops throughout the text: a spatial division paralleling Connie's state in the enclosure of the mansion contrasted with the expanse of the woods. Clifford's writing brings him in contact with an ambitious Irish playwright, Michaelis, an obvious social climber. Michaelis quickly takes an interest in Connie. They begin an affair that is immediately satisfying to both. Although physically uneven in its satisfaction, Connie's mood becomes lighter and in turn Clifford benefits from this change.

More details on the day-to-day life are developed in **Chapter Four.** Lawrence introduces a group of Clifford's friends—Tommy Dukes, Charles May, and Arnold Hammond—who spend their time discussing sex, marriage, and Bolshevism. Connie is an ever present yet silent witness to these conversations since Clifford insists that she accompany him at all times. The prattle of the men's talk sharply contrasts with the silence of Connie's presence. Connie listens to their words but thinks her own thoughts including making a comparison of these men to Michaelis. In **Chapter Five** the sense of enclosure continues and becomes more defined for several reasons. First, Clifford tells Connie that sex means nothing compared to a life-long relationship, an 'integrated life'. (45) He brings up the possibility of Connie having a child by another man—in order to carry on the family name and as long as he does not know the details. Next, Connie first sees Mellors, the new gamekeeper. Later, as the years pass, Clifford's success with his writing increases, as does Connie's own form of paralysis. Her only contact with others is an occasional meeting with Michaelis. Their relationship ends with a brutal attack by Michaelis which leaves Connie devastated and her desire for him or any other destroyed. Connie realizes her only future is Clifford's version of "the integrated life, the long living together of two people who are in the habit of being in the same house with one another. Nothingness!" (55)

At the beginning of **Chapter Six,** Constance questions Tommy Dukes on men and women. His answers offer no real clarification and she retreats, once again, to the wood. There she runs into Mellors and his daughter, who is weeping desperately because her father has just shot a cat. This first encounter is hardly a positive one. As Constance returns home, she ponders how hollow the word 'home' has become and the idea of having a child surfaces again. Later, by chance, Connie comes upon the gamekeeper washing himself at the side of his cottage. The vision stops her in her tracks. She studies the "perfect, white solitary nudity" (66) until she has to move away to collect her thoughts. When she comments later to Clifford that Mellors could pass for a gentleman, he rebuffs the statement with disinterest.

Chapter Seven opens with an essential scene in the depiction of Constance's evolution. As she readies for bed, Connie examines the condition of her naked body in a mirror. Although she is only 27 years old, Connie notices a slacking of the skin much like that of an older woman. The next day her dreary life continues its usual course. A visit from Clifford's Aunt Eva brightens the routine but only temporarily. Recognizing her need for help, Connie writes to Hilda who, upon her arrival at Wragby, is astonished at her sister's state. Hilda takes control, admonishes Clifford for Connie's pathetic condition, arranges for Connie to have medical attention, and most importantly, contracts Mrs. Bolton as Clifford's private nurse. The change in life at Wragby is immediate. Clifford, reluctant at first, soon relinquishes to Mrs. Bolton all the duties of his care, thus freeing Connie from her confinement to the house.

Chapter Eight begins the second phase in Connie's life as Lady Chatterley. Connie walks in the woods to build her strength and senses a new freedom in the outdoors. Following the noise of hammering leads her further into the wood where she finds a secret hut where the gamekeeper raises pheasants. Politely, they exchange a few words. When Mellors notices that Constance is blue with cold, he builds a fire inside where she sits and examines the roughness of the little sanctuary. As Connie warms herself, she remembers the sight of Mellors bathing and compares it to the clothed and brooding man she now observes. Outside, Mellors resents having to come in contact with a woman. As a hired man, he realizes even his solitude is not his own. When Connie asks for a key to the hut, Mellors refuses, trying to protect what little privacy he has. On another walk, she runs into Mellors. They exchange harsh words over the key. Connie is left bewildered by the man.

In **Chapter Nine** Connie develops an aversion to Clifford. At the same time, there is an evolution of trust between Mrs. Bolton and Clifford. In the evenings, Connie now sits silently as these two converse. Slowly, Mrs. Bolton stimulates Clifford's interest in the mines with her stories and gossip. There is a gradual transition in roles between Mrs. Bolton and Constance; Clifford is noticeably stiffer when dealing with his wife than with his nurse. Then, in **Chapter Ten,** Clifford's interest in a newly installed radio increases Connie's sense of isolation. But once again the topic of having a child is discussed. Clifford suggests that science might allow him to have his own child. She retreats to the wood where she runs into a changed Mellors. He has made her a key to the hut. He shows her the hens that he is breeding. Connie is moved and weeps softly. Her tears touch Mellors who reaches out and embraces her. Mellors leads her into the hut where they make love for the first time. When, at length, they speak, they agree they have no regrets but Mellors has concerns about the complications that this 'return to life' represents. Some days later, they meet and make love again. Mellors voices his concerns about the future once more. Mrs. Bolton is suspicious of Constance's outings and thinks she might have a lover. One evening, Mrs. Bolton, having responded to Clifford's calls, looks out a window and discovers Mellors staring up at the mansion, thus identifying Lady Chatterley's lover.

In **Chapter Eleven,** Constance tells Mrs. Bolton about having a child mainly as a ruse for her recent activities. Mrs. Bolton interprets the news as a gift from science and starts the rumor about the child in town. Soon, all around think Clifford still can produce an heir. Then, a ride in the country draws out even more of Connie's desperate thoughts regarding her life at Wragby. Yet she and Mrs. Bolton come closer as Mrs. Bolton shares details of her past with Connie. Mellors and Constance meet in his cottage in **Chapter Twelve.** Initially Mellors reacts harshly to Connie's talk about a baby and he accuses her of wanting him only to "get a child". (169) They talk through this disagreement, reveal their love for each other, and plan to spend the night together. Connie is so transformed by her newly found love that she imitates Mellors' dialect. In **Chapter Thir-**

teen however, a painful scene occurs when Clifford insists on going to the wood in his mechanized wheel chair. During their walk together, Clifford expounds his views on life, social classes and the future to Connie. Increasingly she takes offense at his words. When his chair becomes stuck, Clifford stubbornly refuses her suggestion to seek help. Mellors happens upon them and tries to help. Clifford at first refuses but then "yellow with anger" (190) relents. Exasperated, Clifford accepts Mellors' help but talks loudly to Connie as if to remove Mellor's presence from the scene. She lashes out at Clifford. As they reach the house quarreling, Connie realizes she must rid her mind of such vileness before she meets her lover that night. **Chapter Fourteen** begins when Constance steals away from Wragby. At Mellors' cottage, she immediately notices his wife's portrait hanging above the bed. Mellors removes it after explaining that he hung it there to remind himself how much he hates his wife, Bertha Coutts. Mellors mentions the inevitable complications the future will bring. In an effort to make the world disappear, the two lovers talk and fall asleep quickly after their passion. In the early morning sun, they both explore each other's naked bodies naming their genitals John Thomas and Lady Jane.

A letter from Hilda confirms a trip to Venice in **Chapter Fifteen**. When Constance tells Clifford of her plans, he makes her promise to return to him. Mellors takes the news more evenly. He recounts his life in India and the army and his views on the evils of money. Constance, full of pleasure in the present, runs naked in the rain. As he dries her, Mellors remarks in his thick dialect: "Tha's got the nicest arse of anybody. It's the nicest, nicest woman's arse as is."(222) During the storm, they talk and Mellors reveals that he has begun divorce proceedings. As the rain ends, Mellors gathers up flowers from the wood and covers her naked body in their blue, pink and golden colors. Later, when they head back to Wragby, they discover Mrs. Bolton waiting. **Chapter Sixteen** begins as Clifford interrogates Connie on her absence during the rainstorm. Mrs. Bolton, who now knows all, tries to soothe his ire. Connie, inwardly, is furious that Mrs. Bolton had been sent to follow her. Nevertheless, Connie is able to talk herself out of the confrontation. Hilda's arrival signals the trip to Venice. Connie, in the meantime, has arranged a sign with Mellors: a red or a green shawl will announce if a night together is possible. Hilda, as it turns out, is divorcing her husband. When Connie reveals her relationship with Mellors Hilda reacts unfavorably but becomes a reluctant accomplice to the lovers. Lawrence depicts a night of unbridled passion between the two lovers. As Connie leaves in the early morning hours, she and Mellors make promises for the future but she senses the departure to be like death.

In **Chapter Seventeen** a role reversal between Hilda and Constance becomes clear. Connie assures her sister that she has experienced the love of a real man, something Hilda has never known. Once in Venice at the Villa Esmeralda, Constance realizes that she is pregnant. Although there are other guests staying at the Villa, Connie's attention is held by letters she receives. First, there are many letters from Clifford, but one reveals that Mellors' wife has returned to the village and has started a scandal. Next, Mrs. Bolton's letter provides more details regarding Bertha Coutts' accusations against Mellors. Desperate, Connie writes to Mrs. Bolton asking her to deliver a note to Mellors. The next letter from Clifford is more alarming. When she finally receives Mellors' letter, she learns that Clifford has dismissed him and that the scandal openly mentions Connie.

Chapter Eighteen begins with Connie arranging to meet Mellors in London. She decides to tell her father, Sir Malcolm, of the pregnancy. Then when Mellors and Connie meet, they discuss the baby, their expectations and Bertha Coutts. Mellors sees Sir Malcolm to talk about salvaging Connie's future, but Connie's father is too drunk at the meeting to accomplish much. When Mellors meets with Hilda, he holds his own despite her sharp tone. Finally, they all agree on a plan: Connie will say that she has had an affair with Duncan Forbes, a family friend. Constance's letter to Clifford begins **Chapter Nineteen.** Clifford quickly becomes hysterical at Connie's account of an affair with Forbes and her petition for a divorce. Fortunately, Mrs. Bolton is there to comfort him as Clifford exposes his inner fears and rage—again Lawrence uses the color yellow to describe the fury in his face. Mrs. Bolton handles his crisis deftly and begins to cry first, thus allowing what she calls the man-child to release his grief and weep for himself. As she caresses him close to her bosom, Clifford reacts as the child he has become letting her kiss his body while gazing up at her. Clifford writes to Connie and insists that she meet him at Wragby. When Constance enters the mansion, no longer its mistress but its victim, her conversation with Clifford quickly becomes hateful. A confrontation by Clifford is followed by Connie's revealing the truth about the child's father: "If he could have sprung out of the chair, he would have done so. His face went yellow, and his eyes bulged with disaster as he glared at her." (295) Clifford accuses her of being insane and refuses to divorce Connie. The next morning she leaves Wragby for the last time and travels to Scotland with Hilda. The text of a letter from Mellors ends the chapter and the novel. He has found work on a farm in the country. He reveals that he is frightened by the 'bad times' that await them, but Mellors assures her that the little flame of their love is ever present. He closes "with a hopeful heart" (302) as John Thomas says good night to his Lady Jane. ❀

List of Characters in
Lady Chatterley's Lover

Constance Chatterley: At first resigned to a sterile life with her handicapped husband, Constance seeks solace in the isolation of the woods on the estate. Her life consists of waiting on her husband, being a silent but ever present witness to his conversations on sex and life, and appearing as the faithful and dutiful lady of the manor. A brief dalliance with an ambitious Irishman leaves Lady Chatterley even more depressed. When she is confronted by the presence of the new gamekeeper, her repression at the side of her husband is replaced by the regenerative powers of her daring liaison with Mellors. At first, Constance is drawn to Mellors by a chance sighting of him bathing. Later, the need to experience a full sexual life opens the way to love, both new and dangerous for Constance. Lady Chatterley, willing to live humbly at Mellors' side, plans to escape the confines imposed by her husband and society, only to be discovered and vilified as Mellors had predicted.

Clifford Chatterley: The heir to Wragby Hall, an estate in the Midlands, Clifford weds Constance, shortly before going to war. A battle injury leaves Clifford paralyzed from the waist down. He returns from the war to carry on life as if nothing had happened. Clifford augments his baronet income first by writing and then by throwing himself headlong into the modernization of the estate's coal pits. Clifford, whose physical condition and disposition require that Constance devote all of her time to his care, is obsessed by his love for Constance and yet is blind to the needs of his wife and others.

Oliver Mellors: The estate gamekeeper, Mellors has returned from the Army where, while stationed in India, he received a field commission as a Lieutenant. Unlike most estate workers, Mellors has education and can cross over from one social group to another. Mellors joined the army after prolonged difficulties with a wandering wife who, late in the novel, circulates the rumor that Mellors receives women in his gamekeeper's cottage. Originally a collier's son from TeObservershall, Mellors speaks in a thick dialect when addressing Clifford but is capable of speaking like any other gentleman. Outwardly remote and sometimes gruff, Mellors shows the tender and loving side of his character as the relationship with Connie evolves. Unlike

Clifford, Mellors has no desire for riches, but seeks peace in the solitude of the woods, knowing all along that the world will invade, discover their affair, and condemn them both.

Mrs. Bolton: The widow of a Tevershall collier killed in a mining accident, she comes to care for Clifford when Hilda and Sir Malcolm deem that Clifford is too much for Constance to manage on her own. Mrs. Bolton takes to her job favorably despite harboring a resentment toward Clifford and his class for unjust accusations made years earlier against her husband. She treats Clifford like the child he really is, gains his confidence and ultimately his version of love. She discovers early on that Constance has a lover and is amazed but not surprised that it is Mellors.

Hilda: Constance's sister, much against her character, weds a man ten years her senior at the time of Constance's marriage to Clifford. Hilda appears at the most desperate times in Constance's life to rescue Constance from her circumstances. Throughout the course of Constance's marriage, Hilda sees that Constance gets medical attention, deals with Clifford directly and harshly, and finally, arranges for Constance to spend one last night with Mellors.

Sir Malcolm Reid: Constance's father, like his daughter Hilda, deals with facts in a straightforward and often brusque manner. Sir Malcolm confronts Clifford about his physical limitations which preclude an heir and keep his daughter a 'demi-vierge'. Yet when Sir Malcolm must face Mellors regarding the scandal and his daughter's involvement, he speaks crudely and only after imbibing several strong drinks.

Michaelis: Despite his apartment in Mayfair and his Bond Street gentlemanly image, he remains an Irishman among English gentry. Michaelis, as an ambitious playwright, initially contacts Clifford, but becomes Connie's first lover, satisfying her at the onset of their relationship which sours and leaves her more hopeless than before.

Tommy Dukes: One of Clifford's friends, Dukes regularly dines with Clifford and his other male friends who discuss sex, bolshevism, and life. He is a Clifford without the paralysis whose views represent those of his generation and class. ❦

Critical Views on
Lady Chatterley's Lover

Letter from D. H. Lawrence to Nelly Morrison

[Nelly Morrison agreed to type the manuscript of *Lady Chatterley's Lover*. In this letter Lawrence responds after Ms. Morrison changes her mind because she finds the content distasteful. Lawrence understands and forgives her change of heart but not her opinion.]

To Nelly Morrison, from Villa Mirenda, Scandicci,
8 January 1928

Dear Nelly Morrison: I wasn't surprised when I got your letter, had rather expected it before. I felt, almost as soon as I'd given you the MS. that I had made a mistake. It's my fault entirely, not yours: to me the blame, not you.

It was very kind of you to have done so much, to have gone on, feeling as you say you did about it, just because of your friendship for me.

And remember, although you are on the side of the angels and the vast majority, I consider mine is the truly moral and religious position. You suggest I have pandered to the pornographic taste: I think not. To the Puritan all things are impure, to quote an Americanism. Not that you are a Puritan: nor am I impure.

I'll call shortly and relieve you of the MS. What a mercy you haven't seen the rest! I finished it today.

Every man his own taste: every woman her own distaste. But don't try to ride a moral horse: it could be nothing but a sorry ass.

All the same I am awfully grateful to you for having done as much as you did, and am really sorry I asked you to do something so distasteful to you. You must forgive me for that.

Meanwhile, for heaven's sake, don't do any more. Pack the thing up for me when I call, I hope Tuesday or Wednesday. Then let us forget the whole show, stand as we did before, and leave the recording angel to write the last word.

—D. H. Lawrence, "Letter to Nelly Morrison." In *The Collected Letters of D. H. Lawrence,* Volume 2, ed. Henry T. Moore (New York: Viking, 1962): pp. 1032–1033.

Carl Bedient on the Radicalism of *Lady Chatterley's Lover*

[Professor Bedient, the author of *Architects of the Self: George Eliot, D. H. Lawrence, and E. M. Forster* (1972) has also published a volume of poetry entitled *Candy Necklace* (1997). In this early critical work on Lawrence's controversial novel, Bedient contends that the critics of that time period emasculate Lawrence. In this except, Bedient wishes to look closer at the ambiguities of the text and examines here two of three titles Lawrence used for the different versions of the novel: *Tenderness* and *John Thomas and Lady Jane.*]

One way of approaching the ambiguities of the book, of discovering, beneath its "love story," the Lawrencian explosive, is to consider the appropriateness of its three projected titles: *Tenderness*; Lawrence's final choice, *John Thomas and Lady Jane*; and his publishers' preference, *Lady Chatterley's Lover*. As it happens, in each case the appropriateness is ambiguous—a sign of the novel's relative richness in the Lawrence canon.

Of the three titles, *Tenderness* is perhaps preferable. The tenderness of this book, so overwhelming, so surprising in view of the earlier work, so perfect a gift from a dying man, is self-luminous, and not only aesthetic and physical, the overflow of delight, but human, born of compassion. It is an aesthetic tenderness, the grace and virtue of senses and of a sensibility open to the poetry of this world, that hears and reports "the tinkle as of tiny water-bells" of John's Well, that lingers over the first violets "that smelled sweet and cold, sweet and cold," that sees the daffodils "rustling and fluttering and shivering, so bright and alive," the "thick-clustered primroses no longer shy." And it is a tenderness of the body, the glow that radiates from the sense of touch, from the aroused blood, that warms many passages of the book. But what is new in the range of this tenderness—new enough to be revolutionary—is a quite human tenderness, that is, a moral one. Hitherto Lawrence had allowed in his scheme of salvation no place at all for Agape, for the milder Eros, for love not experienced "in extremity"—for a love that was not a strife between "polarities" but a corroboration and a celebration of being. But in *Lady Chatterley's Lover* he has brought together for the first time the two great streams of sensuality and affection. Compassion and passion become subtle translations of each other, as when Mellors, before the pheasant coops, seeing a tear fall onto Connie's wrist, "stood up, and stood away, moving to the other coop. For suddenly he was aware of the old flame shooting and leaping up in his loins, that he had hoped was quiescent for ever." It is a high moment in Lawrence's art, indeed in English literature, this moment of passionate tenderness; with St. Augustine, it says *I want you to be.*

It is Mellors, however, who says of "the Cliffords and Berthas":

> Tender to them? Yea, even then the tenderest thing you could do for them, perhaps, would be to give them death. They can't live. They only frustrate life. . . . Death ought to be sweet to them. And I ought to be allowed to shoot them.

This is the old, too-familiar Lawrencian arrogance—the arrogance that was so virulent a combination of egoism and fear of the world. Clifford himself later says of Mellors: "You'd wonder . . . that such beings were ever allowed to be born." Between the two, what is there to choose? And in quite a different way, the tenderness of the novel is complicated by the curiously belated, rather hollow, brief emphasis on the "piercing thrills of sensuality, different, sharper, more terrible than the thrills of tenderness. . . ." To Connie's dazed question, "But you'll keep the tenderness for me, won't you?" Mellors responds only by a kiss and a momentary embrace. Connie pities Hilda for having never known "either real tenderness or real sensuality"; and "the supreme pleasure of the mind," it is said, is nothing to "sheer fiery sensuality," which, in fact, is necessary "to purify and quicken the mind." All this is I think, a willed, half-hearted, incomplete eruption into a novel not really particularly sympathetic to it of the old Lawrencian Eros, which was violent, extreme, and dehumanizing. Now, it is not the presence of the old deity here, but its discomfort, that is significant. Yet both the murderous lack of charity and the stress on *sheer* sensuality have a common root: Lawrence's fear and hatred of the individual *person.* And the continued, felt force in Lawrence's last novel of this abiding antipathy leads to the questions: Was Lawrence not right to want to call his novel *John Thomas and Lady Jane*? Or are Mellors and Connie, despite all, the true hero and heroine?

    —Carl Bedient, "The Radicalism of *Lady Chatterley's Lover*," *The Hudson Review* 19, no. 3 (New York, 1966): pp. 408–410.

CHARLES M. BURACK ON THE ASSAULT ON VERBAL AND VISUAL CONSCIOUSNESS

> [Burack, from the University of California at Berkeley, concentrates in this essay on Lawrence's technique in light of reader response. He contends that Lawrence alters the reader's consciousness and orientation to self and the world. In this excerpt, Burack focuses on chapter I where the narrator describes, in the language of science, Connie and Hilda's experiences and beliefs regarding sex.]

Throughout Chapter 1, the narrator uses the language of science to satirize young Connie and Hilda and parody the omnipresent scientistic mindset. Scientific discourse emphasizes categorization, explanation, prediction and control. The overuse of abstract words, compound-terms and noun phrases suggests that the sisters' erotic experiences have been filtered, reduced and governed by their rational minds. What "mattered supremely" to Connie and Hilda was not "the sex thing" or "love experience" but "the impassioned interchange of talk." "Sex thing" suggests the scientific tendency to objectify phenomena, and "impassioned interchange of talk" reads like jargon from a social psychology textbook. Hyphenated phrases like "sex-thrill" and "love-making" resemble chemical compounds, and the hyphen accentuates the dualism built into scientific thought. The plethora of conjoined abstract nouns is precisely what George Orwell will later identify as one of the "mental vices" of writers living in an age wedded to scientific abstractions and political orthodoxy. In *Lady Chatterley,* the continued repetition of these abstract phrases is intended to have an annoying effect on readers. This annoyance could intensify to anger or modulate to boredom.

In fact, the narrator repeats "sex" ad nauseam in order to indicate its nearly null meaning and to further negate any lingering sense. In two short, successive paragraphs, "sex" is repeated six times: "sex business . . . sexual love . . . sex thing . . . sex . . . sex thing . . . sexual intercourse." The insistent repetition acts like the blows of Mellors' hammer that startle and shatter Connie's consciousness. In Chapter 6, "sex" is said to be one of "the great words" that, "it seemed to Connie, were cancelled for her generation." The novel's destruction phase tries to cancel out the dead or deadening meanings of these once great words so that they can be later invested with some of the religious power of pagan fertility rites. In short, "sex" will be redefined, revalued and recharged in the erotic scenes involving Connie and Mellors. The repetitions of "sex" also indicate the ubiquitous presence of this term in scientific and popular discourse during the first decades of the century.

To the sisters' scientific minds, the words "sex" and "love" are so abstract and empty that their semantic differences are almost nonexistent. The narrator reinforces the sense of interchangeability by placing the words in alternating paragraphs: "It was obvious in them too that love had gone through them: that is, the physical experience. . . . In the actual sex thrill within the body, the sisters nearly succumbed." Sex and love have been reduced not only to each other but also to a "physical experience." That is, their meanings have been limited to those assigned by the mechanistically-oriented physical sciences. Lawrence tends to use the adjective "sensual" rather than "physical" when valorizing an unselfconscious bodily experience; he sometimes uses "sensuous" to describe the self-conscious, physical experiences that he deplores. Freud had hoped to reduce psychoanalysis to a physiological science, expressing this aim as early as 1895 in "Psychology for Neurologists" and as late as 1920 in *Beyond the Pleasure Principle*. P. D. Ouspensky, an important influence on Lawrence's understanding of the relations among religion, science, and philosophy, considered physicalism the defining characteristic of positivist science: "positivism looks for causes of biological and psychological phenomena in physico-mechanical phenomena."

A scientific or commercial consciousness that can lump diverse phenomena is itself lumpable—that is, generic and therefore fungible. In fact, the narrator lumps Connie and Hilda together as he describes their sexual behavior. In thirteen successive paragraphs the girls are usually treated in the plural: "They had to be taken to Paris and Florence . . . So they had given the gift of themselves . . . Both sisters had had their love experience . . . They loved their respective young men . . . In the actual sex thrill within the body, the sisters nearly succumbed." The extensive use of summary in these paragraphs also suggests the abstractness of the sisters' lives. In effect, the narrator presents the scientific "results" and "conclusions" of their teenage years. This general tendency toward abstraction reinforces the reduction, and thus assists the subjugation, of women. The abstractness and interchangeability of the sisters' experiences also suggest that they and their experiences have become commodified. Even the modern woman is portrayed as a commodity: Tommy Dukes, a spokesman for Lawrence, criticizes Arnold Hammond for allowing his "strong property instinct" to govern his relationship with his wife Julia, who "is labelled *Mrs. Arnold B. Hammond.*" Lawrence thus links the categorizations and reifications in science to those in business.

Minds wedded to naming things come to love words more than the things they represent, to prefer talk to action, and to use language to exploit people. The narrator emphasizes the sisters' logocentric preference for intellectual discourse over sex, which is considered "only a sort of primitive reversion and a bit of an anticlimax." Words are so important to Connie and Hilda that they require verbal engagement before they can be sexually aroused, for neither is "ever in love with a young man unless he and she were verbally very near: that is unless they were profoundly interested, TALKING to one another." Words are thus conceptual tools that induce or coerce a physical response. The instrumental value of words is related to the instrumental value of sex partners, who are "merely her tool" for achieving orgasm. In current theoretical terms, the manmade logos that subjugates women's bodies and experiences can also be used by women to control men; it is a weapon in the hands of either sex. Yet when the word dominates in sexuality, all suffer.

—Charles Burack, "Mortifying the Reader: The Assault on Verbal and Visual Consciousness in D. H. Lawrence's *Lady Chatterley's Lover,*" *Studies in the Novel* 29, no. 4 (University of North Texas, 1997): pp. 496–498.

John B. Humma on Metaphor and Meaning

> [Besides this book, John Humma has published several critical essays on Lawrence along with articles on Sir Walter Scott and John Fowles. In the chapter entitled "The Interpenetrating Metaphor: Nature and Myth in *Lady Chatterley's Lover*," Humma considers how Lawrence uses nature imagery to serve his purposes. Humma here compares nature imagery in *Lady Chatterley's Lover* with that in *Women in Love* and *Aaron's Rod* by focusing on flowers, in particular the lily.]

To compare *Lady Chatterley* with other Lawrence novels is to appreciate the unique strategic function of the nature imagery here. Although Lawrence's reputation for describing nature is deservedly high, the general view is that *Lady Chatterley's Lover* marks a falling off. Harry T. Moore's criticism is probably representative: "Nature appears fairly frequently in *Lady Chatterley's Lover*, though not so effectively as in previous novels; if Lawrence's descriptive powers had been at their height when he was writing *Lady Chatterley*, it would have made a far more forceful book." As Moore acknowledges, however, Lawrence could still write nature passages charged with color, as is evident from the nature descriptions generally in the late works. But we do not quite expect from *Lady Chatterley* the almost unearthly "nature" scenes that somehow came from his pen in *The Rainbow* and *Women in Love*. The confrontation between Ursula and the horses late in the first novel and the "Moony" episode in the second are scenes, one feels, that Lawrence could not have *not* written, scenes that his daimon wrote, so to speak, though this is not to deny the shaping hand its part. In contrast, *Lady Chatterley* offers a thoughtful subordination of nature to the structure of meaning, an orchestration of detail that is purely the achievement of sullen craft.

What have been symbols in previous Lawrence novels become metaphors here. When Ursula passes through the wood near Willey Water before encountering the horses in the meadow, the trees are symbolic, not metaphoric. In *Lady Chatterley's Lover* the trees are, of course, both. The "commemorating" cypresses of *Aaron's Rod* are symbols, as are the eagles in their dalliance and the lily:

> Happy lily, never to be saddled with an *idée fixe*, never to be in the grip of a monomania for happiness or love or fulfilment. It is not *laisser aller*. It is life-rootedness. It is being by oneself, life-living, like the much-mooted lily. One toils, one spins, one strives: just as the lily does. But like her, taking one's own life-way amidst everything, and taking one's own life-way alone. Love too. But there also, taking one's way alone, happily alone in all the wonders of communion, swept up on the winds, but never swept away from one's very self. Two eagles in mid-air, maybe, like Whitman's "Dalliance of Eagles." Two eagles in mid-air grappling, whirling, coming to their intensification of love-oneness there in mid-air. In mid-air the love consummation. But all the time each lifted on its own wings: each bearing itself up on its own wings at every moment of the mid-air love consummation. That is the splendid love-way.

Here the eagles and the lily merely symbolize the ethic that Lilly embodies. Obviously, though, Lawrence also uses images metaphorically, as in this passage from *Aaron's Rod*:

> Sunlight, lovely full sunlight, lingered warm and still on the balcony. It caught the facade of the cathedral sideways, like the tips of a flower, and sideways lit up the stem of Giotto's tower, like a lily stem, or a long, lovely pale pink and white and green pistil of the lily of the cathedral. Florence, the flowery town. Firenze—Fiorenze—the flowery town: the red lilies. The Fiorentini, the flower-souled. Flowers with good roots in the mud and muck, as should be: and fearless blossoms in air, like the cathedral and the tower and the David.

The lily figure serves the passage but, unlike the figures in *Lady Chatterley's Lover*, does not serve in any fully orchestrated way the central action of the story. It is primarily a mechanical component, not an organic one. We even find a metaphor within a metaphor, as in *Lady Chatterley*: "But I love it; it is delicate and rosy, and the dark stripes are as they should be, like the tiger marks on a pink lily. It's a lily, not a rose: a pinky white lily with dark tigery marks." But the metaphors only feather, they do not interlock; we find no meshing of meaning, no engagement with prior or subsequent details. *Lady Chatterley* and *The Escaped Cock* are the mature achievements of the narrative technique that, as we have seen, had its beginnings in *Aaron's Rod*.

In the "Excurse" chapter of *Women in Love*, after Ursula and Birkin resolve their quarrel, Birkin is said to feel "as if he had just come awake, like a thing that is born, like a bird when it comes out of its egg, into a new universe." At the inn they speak only through "the flowers in each other"; the strange passage in which Ursula kneels before Birkin incorporates river, flood, and fountain images. At the end of the chapter, they walk among "the great old trees" of Sherwood Forest, where, "like old priests," the fern rises in the distance, "magical and mysterious." Like Mellors and Connie, Birkin and Ursula make love on the floor of the wood. But in this passage, unlike the one from *Lady Chatterley's Lover*, which I examine below, Lawrence provides no nature imagery at all. In short, although he gives us the vegetable, animal, and water imagery of previous parts of the chapter and endows the wood with a religious aura, we do not find any sort of organic interpenetration involving the images and the action. My point, of course, is not that there is anything amiss with his treatment of the scene here, or with his treatment of those in *Aaron's Rod*; it is simply that the absence of such a strategy in these novels and others points up the deliberate orchestration of the nature details in *Lady Chatterley's Lover*. What allows for it here, if not dictates it, is the blatantly phallic action. The orchestration is simply a matter of Lawrence's having found what suffices for him.

—John B. Humma, *Metaphor and Meaning in D. H. Lawrence's Later Novels* (Columbia: University of Missouri Press, 1990): pp. 90–92.

Aldous Huxley: D. H. Lawrence in *The Olive Tree*

[In this essay by the eminent author of canonical works such as *Brave New World* and *Point Counter Point*, Huxley discusses the friendship he enjoyed with Lawrence and the genius of Lawrence. In this excerpt, Huxley suggests that Lawrence's gift caused him to feel isolated which in turn may have explained his "wanderings round the earth." Huxley comments on *Lady Chatterley's Lover* as a reflection of the author's sad life.]

⟨. . .⟩ Of all the possible words of disparagement which might be applied to our uneasy age "personal" is surely about the last that would occur to most of us. To Lawrence it was the first. His gift was a gift of feeling and rendering the unknown, the mysteriously other. To one possessed by such a gift, almost any age would have seemed unduly and dangerously personal. He had to reject and escape. But when he had escaped, he could not help deploring the absence of "real human relationships." Spasmodically, he tried to establish contact with the body of mankind. There were the recurrent projects for colonies in remote corners of the earth; they all fell through. . . .

It was, I think, the sense of being cut off that sent Lawrence on his restless wanderings round the earth. His travels were at once a flight and a search: a search for some society with which he could establish contact, for a world where the times were not personal and conscious knowing had not yet perverted living; a search and at the same time a flight from the miseries and evils of the society into which he had been born, and for which, in spite of his artist's detachment, he could not help feeling profoundly responsible. He felt himself "English in the teeth of all the world, even in the teeth of England": that was why he had to go to Ceylon and Australia and Mexico. He could not have felt so intensely English in England without involving himself in corporative political action, without belonging and being attached; but to attach himself was something he could not bring himself to do, something that the artist in him felt as a violation. He was at once too English and too intensely an artist to stay at home. "Perhaps it is necessary for me to try these places, perhaps it is my destiny to know the world. It only excites the outside of me. The inside it leaves more isolated and stoic than ever. That's how it is. It is all a form of running away from oneself and the great problems, all this wild west and the strange Australia. But I try to keep quite clear. One forms not the faintest inward attachment, especially here in America."

His search was as fruitless as his flight was ineffective. He could not escape either from his homesickness or his sense of responsibility; and he never found a society to which he could belong. In a kind of despair, he plunged yet deeper into the surrounding mystery, into the dark night of that otherness whose essence and symbol is the sexual experience. In *Lady Chatterley's Lover* Lawrence wrote the epilogue to his travels and, from his long and fruitless experience of flight and search, drew what was, for him, the inevitable moral. It is a strange and beautiful book; but inexpressibly sad. But then so, at bottom, was its author's life.

—Aldous Huxley, "D. H. Lawrence in *The Olive Tree*." In *Collected Essays* (New York: Harper & Brothers Publishers, 1959): pp. 125–126.

BARRY J. SCHERR ON LAWRENTIAN *DAEMONIZATION* AND *ASKESIS*

[Along with this critical study, Barry Scherr has published extensively on D. H. Lawrence. Scherr's premise maintains that critics have dealt little with Lawrence's self-esteem and its impact on his work or on Lawrence's relation to Plato. In the chapter entitled "Lawrentian *Daemonization* and *Askesis*," Scherr bases his arguments on the attacks Lawrence made on Plato in his non-fiction writing and on two concepts developed by Harold Bloom: *daemonization* and *askesis*. In this excerpt, Scherr examines the Lawrentian *askesis* he sees in Lady Chatterley's Lover.]

In *Lady Chatterley's Lover* the Lawrentian *askesis* is presented not only by Lawrence as omniscient author, but also by several Lawrentian spokesmen in the novel. One minor spokesman of the Lawrentian "phallic consciousness" in the novel, Tommy Dukes, declares that "our civilization is going to fall. It's going down the bottomless pit, down the chasm. And, believe me, the only bridge across the chasm will be the phallus!"; and he adds: "Give me the democracy of touch, the resurrection of the body!" Tommy Dukes' statements here are certainly reminiscent of Lawrence's pronouncements about the "phallic regeneration" of England in his essay "A Propos of *Lady Chatterley's Lover*," in which Lawrence asserts his belief that it is imperative for England to have a "phallic regeneration" that is the product of "a proper reverence for sex, and a proper awe of the body's strange experience"—a regeneration in which "the bridge to the future is the phallus."

But Tommy Dukes is all talk and no action as a representative of the phallic consciousness; he is essentially nothing more than a loquacious celibate. "I neither marry nor run after women," he says. "I go to bed by myself; and am none the worse for it." Tommy Dukes, though he speaks about the "phallic" realm of touch and the body, does not actively participate in that realm; Mellors, on the other hand, the main Lawrentian spokesman of *Lady Chatterley's Lover*, enthusiastically participates in the realm of touch and the body with Connie Chatterley.

While Tommy Dukes merely verbalizes the Lawrentian version of *askesis* in *Lady Chatterley's Lover*, Mellors is the effective exemplar, in word and deed, of the Lawrentian *askesis*. Like Lawrence, Mellors regards touch in general and sex in particular as the ultimate activities:

> Then with a quiver of exquisite pleasure he [Mellors] touched the warm soft body [of Connie Chatterley]. . . . And he had to come into her at once, to enter the peace on earth of her soft, quiescent body. It was the moment of pure peace for him, the entry into the body of a woman.

A little later in the novel Mellors ardently tells Connie Chatterley: "I could die for the touch of a woman like thee"; thus, for Mellors, sex and touch are more important than life itself—indeed, sex is life itself to Mellors-Lawrence as he experiences a feeling of reverence for the female orgasm during the sexual climax of Connie Chatterley with Mellors in the fir-tree forest:

> . . . she lay there crying in unconscious inarticulate cries [of orgasm]. The voice out of the uttermost night, the life! The man [Mellors] heard it beneath him with a kind of awe, as his life sprang out into her.

This is Connie Chatterley's first experience of orgasmic sex with Mellors; furthermore, it is the first time in her life that Connie Chatterley achieves simultaneous orgasm with a lover. Lawrence's main spokesman Mellors places great emphasis on the achievement of simultaneous orgasm:

> "We came off together that time," he said.
> She did not answer.
> "It's good when it's like that. Most folks live their lives through and they never know it [simultaneous orgasm]," he said, speaking rather dreamily.

Thus, in his extreme emphasis on "the *body's* strange experience" in sex, Lawrence is no longer content to depict the psychic and emotional complexities in the sexual relationship, but now feels compelled to describe the veritable sexual act itself, even to the extent of specifying the precise nature of the sexual response of his characters; accordingly, in *Lady Chatterley's Lover* Lawrence tells us exactly what type of orgasm is taking place in his characters, with his spokesman Mellors voicing his (Lawrence's) belief that the simultaneous orgasm should be privileged over all other modes of sexual response.

—Barry J. Scherr, *D. H. Lawrence's Response to Plato: A Bloomian Interpretation* (New York: Peter Lang): pp. 122–123.

CAROL SIEGEL ON LAWRENCE'S RESPONSES TO HIS FEMALE PRECURSORS

[Professor Siegel has published, along with the present book, *Male Masochism: Modern Revisions of the Story of Love* (1995) as well as essays on Postmodern women novelists and Victorian literature. This chapter uses the perspective of intertextuality and feminist criticism. In this excerpt, Professor Siegel explains how Lawrence's text responds to works by the Brontë sisters: *Jane Eyre* and *Wuthering Heights*.]

The most striking differences between Charlotte Brontë's concept of womanly rage and that of Emily Brontë (and Lawrence) is that the former, in *Jane Eyre,* allows compromise not only with reality but with Victorian morality. Emily Brontë illustrates both society's demand that women repress their anger or die *and* the evil that results from obeying that demand; Charlotte Brontë intercedes for her heroine and thus strongly suggests that suppression of anger will be rewarded with a kind of divine intervention. The circumstances of the resolution of Jane's romantic problem imply that submission to socializing forces must precede the successful call and even that woman's anger must be transferred outside herself and destroyed before fulfillment can be achieved. When Jane learns to "regulate [her] mind," providence takes her part and releases her mind's fires. It is not simply to allow Jane's marriage that Bertha is destroyed. As many critics have noted, Bertha is Jane's double in that she incarnates the furious rebelliousness against patriarchal control that Jane learns to repress as she matures. Before Jane can achieve her happiness, her anger, exteriorized as both Rochester's rejection of Christian morality and Bertha's entire being, must be killed.

Although it is clear from a great many of Lawrence's poems and essays that he was attracted by the idea of curing women's rage into quiet submissiveness, he seems unwilling to dramatize such a resolution in his fiction. Even when he sets the stage to show a woman's taming, the conflict between the sexes is projected beyond the novel's closing; the angry voices of his women seem likely to continue being heard. Ursula in *Women in Love,* March in *The Fox,* Hannele in *The Captain's Doll,* Harriet in *Kangaroo,* and Kate in *The Plumed Serpent* never give in to their lovers' demands for their submission. In "Mother and Daughter" and "The Woman Who Rode Away," which depict heroines who do submit, the specific acts of female submission paradoxically express anger and rebellion. Through her engagement to the fatherly Arnault, Virginia Bodoin is finally able to strike back against her mother, who has always treated her as her "*alter ego,* her other self." The woman who rides away is in furious rebellion against just such a husband as Arnault. "Like any sheikh," he isolates her, "sway[s] her, down[s] her, [keeps] her in an invincible slavery" until she, realizing she is "dead already," allows the Indians to sacrifice her in a ritual to destroy the white man's world. When Lawrence gives up the idea of male leadership and organized revolt, he also seems to give up this idea of a woman rebelling against one patriarchal system by surrendering to another, and when he deals at great length with *Jane Eyre,* in the second version of *Lady Chatterley's Lover,* he seems determined to show that Jane should have been mated to the signifier and agent of female anger, Heathcliff, rather than buried in Victorian niceness with the safely crippled Rochester. Lawrence's rewriting of Charlotte Brontë's story reveals that what really disturbed him about *Jane Eyre* was the taming of Jane through resolution of her rage, not the maiming of Rochester through which her rage was resolved.

The figure who represents Jane's rage is given an important role in the second version of *Lady Chatterley's Lover, John Thomas and Lady Jane*. Higdon has convincingly demonstrated that Lawrence's Bertha Coutts, the estranged wife of the gamekeeper, was derived from Bertha Mason. Their lives, habits, and attitudes are remarkably similar, and Bertha Coutts is even described as being "like a mad-woman." But, while *Jane Eyre* tells us very little that can excite sympathy for Bertha Mason, Connie blames Parkin's insufficiencies for driving her rival "evil-mad." Connie's musings about the marriage-maddened Bertha recall Cathy Earnshaw, who also "fought against even the love in her own soul." Lawrence, like Emily Brontë (and Jean Rhys), finds the explanation of the wife's insanity in her situation as wife—in the situation of any wife—subject through marriage to the demands of a patriarchal order that denies her femaleness. Moreover, Lawrence, like Brontë, keeps this specter of female rage alive. If Bertha stands in for Cathy's angry ghost, Connie is no civilized and repressed Catherine Linton. Like Cathy (or Jane in her childhood), the Connie of *John Thomas and Lady Jane* exults in her own rage. Her anger, again like that of both heroines, arises from her condition as a woman. "She [is] angry, angry at the implied insult to womanhood" not once but often throughout the novel. Like Jane and Cathy she finds an angry, rebellious lover, but unlike them she understands that his fury is "part of her own revolt." The intermingling of angry voices destroys the false "Paradise of wealth and well-being" available to Connie at Wragby Hall, but destroys nothing in the two lovers except artificial gender identities built up around their true selves by society. Yet the Eden is still contained within the male order; its existence seems to depend on open female revolt against that order.

Lawrence's responses to *Wuthering Heights* and the novels he felt were influenced by it suggest that to him the tragedy in their shared theme adheres not in woman's (or man's) circumstances, but in the cultural inscription of repression and denial of uncivilized female passions, as if anger, fierceness, and violence could be separated out of sexual relations by the simple addition of sweet femininity. To Lawrence, Cathy represents the aspect of Brontë (he might call it her daemon—her essential self) that needs the body, no matter how imprisoning marriage and pregnancy make it seem to her, to make possible revitalizing contact with the natural world through man. He interprets Cathy's longing for death as the mark of Heathcliff's failure to bring her fulfillment and so creates Heathcliffs of his own who can better answer the call that he heard in women's fiction, that he imagined coming from her core self.

Lawrence's impulse to rewrite *Wuthering Heights* was naïve. Brontë's discontent is of another sort than that which proposes worldly solutions. Despite her enumeration of injustices in property laws, she seems ultimately above concern with social change, although not above gender chauvinism. In *Wuthering Heights,* she values woman's natural passions above all else, and disdains everything, including woman's own fertility, that interferes with the expression of those passions. What gives Cathy her stature is her refusal to accept any compromise, her refusal to control herself in any way. For Brontë such refusal necessitates death, although the tone of *Wuthering Heights'* conclusion reveals her regret that this must be. Olive Schreiner and George Eliot (at least in *The Mill on the Floss*) fatalistically value death as the only possible release from the conflict between the demands of passion and civilization, a conflict that rends humans in two. Charlotte Brontë seems to believe that the death of anger is a possible solution and proposes killing it by killing male power.

Lawrence, however, sees the male consciousness as the ground on which female wholeness can be achieved. If *Wuthering Heights* is the wild female call, he cannot see the assertions of feminine victimization and virtue presented in *The Story of an African Farm, The Mill on the Floss,* and *Jane Eyre* as valuable answers. To Lawrence, man "alone of the two, perhaps, can dimly apprehend the whole of the dream" of passion; woman, who can only appreciate man as her "pure ecstatic servant," does not understand that his effectiveness in that role depends on his ability to "read" her. Consequently, Lawrence's high valuation of female passion is always accompanied by implied or explicit exhortations to men to interpret it for the women who feel it. His ideal union depends on both the woman's anger ("like discernable fire"), which energizes sexuality, and the male's "higher understanding," which makes her "acknowledge him as a sort of fate, her own fate."

Lawrence begins to move back across the border between gendered texts when he goes from finding an ideology through Brontë to speaking as or for her. In apparent reaction to his recognition of the necessity of the female voice and audience to his own existence as an author, he insists on the necessity of man to woman. If his women generally found their female voices issuing from the throats of men and asserting men's importance, as Daphne does, Lawrence would make us understand Brontë's femaleness only by contrast. The confrontation between their texts would have the look of war and its crossfire would show us the hard outlines of a textual gender specificity without shading. Instead, Lawrence's virtual compulsion to give voice to female anger that resists appropriation and undercuts his assertion of the value of man, even as he speaks it, makes the border waver. Although in this respect Lawrence's new heaven and earth have in common with the old ones dependence on a masculine hermeneutics, the world of Lawrence's fiction is almost always a return to the world of *Wuthering Heights* before the first sighting of the Lintons: female anger and revolt flourishing in the interstics of patriarchal power.

—Carol Siegel, *Lawrence Among the Women: Wavering Boundaries in Women's Literary Traditions* (Charlottesville: University of Virginia Press, 1991): pp. 84–87.

STANLEY SULTAN ON LAWRENCE THE ANTI-AUTOBIOGRAPHER

[Sultan's most recent book is *Eliot, Joyce and Company* (1990). He has also published short stories of his own as well as critical articles on Renaissance drama. In this essay, Professor Sultan wishes to debunk the standing view by critics that Lawrence's work is highly autobiographical. To do this, he looks at *The White Peacock* and *Sons and Lovers* in particular. But in this excerpt, Sultan examines the gamekeeper's hut, as seen in *The White Peacock* and *Lady Chatterley's Lover,* to provide a textual support for his argument in conjunction with comments made by Jessie Chambers, Lawrence's first love interest.]

A detail that grew in significance and so is of a wholly different order is a gamekeeper's hut. When Chambers wrote of her initial objection to Annable, the gamekeeper in *The White Peacock,* she remarked that

"Lawrence's extraordinary obsession with gamekeepers is difficult to account for" and described "[t]he only encounter" with one he had had during their "acquaintance": when he was seventeen, a gamekeeper required a party of the two of them, her three brothers and his sister Ada to leave some primroses which they had picked.

Setting aside Chambers' assumption that a recurring element in Lawrence's fiction must be "account[ed] for" biographically, her presumption that he had no "encounter" when young in which she did not share seems mistaken. Worthen quotes Burrows telling of Lawrence during those years (while in college) intimidating a gamekeeper socially. And Chambers seems unaware that her sister had shown him a gamekeeper's hut while he was in high school (before he turned sixteen). According to May Holbrook's account, he asked her to show him High Park Wood near his family's farm; she demurred "because it was like showing my heart," and asked "'Did you see the violets?'" In responding, he said that he had been "'careful not to tread on any'"; and then she offered to "'show you the most secret spot in the wood for that.'" She took him to "a tiny clearing where stood a little pavilion of poles"; his "eyes widened with amazement"; and to his "whispered" question, "'what is it?,'" she responded in a whisper, "'the keepers' hut.'"

> —Stanley Sultan, "Lawrence the Anti-Autobiography," *Journal of Modern Literature* 23, no. 2 (Bloomington, Indiana, 1999): pp. 244–245

Works by D. H. Lawrence

The White Peacock. New York: Duffield. 1911; London: Heinemann. 1911.

The Trespasser. London: Duckworth. 1912.

Sons and Lovers. London: Duckworth. 1913.

The Rainbow. London: Methuen.1915.

The Lost Girl. London: Secker. 1920.

Women in Love. New York: Seltzer. 1920; London: Secker. 1921.

Aaron's Rod. New York: Seltzer, 1922. London: Secker. 1922.

The Captain's Doll. London: Secker. 1923.

Kangaroo. London: Secker. 1923.

The Boy in the Bush. London: Secker. 1924.

St. Mawr (Together with The Princess). London: Secker. 1925.

The Plumed Serpent. London: Secker. 1926.

Lady Chatterley's Lover. Florence: Orioli. 1928.

The Virgin and the Gypsy. Florence: Orioli. 1930; Secker. 1930.

Apropos of Lady Chatterley's Lover. London: Mandrake Press. 1930.

Love Among the Haystacks and Other Pieces. London: Nonesuch. 1930.

Works About D. H. Lawrence

Adelman, Gary. *Snow of Fire: Symbolic Meaning in* 'The Rainbow' *and* 'Women in Love'. New York: Garland, 1991.

Bell, Michael. *D. H. Lawrence: Language and Being.* Cambridge: Cambridge University Press, 1992.

Ben-Ephraim, Gavriel. *The Moon's Dominion: Narrative Dichotomy and Female Dominance in Lawrence's Earlier Novels.* London: Associated University Presses, 1981.

Bloom, Harold, ed. *D. H. Lawrence.* New York: Chelsea House Publishers, 1986.

Boulton, James T., ed. *The Letters of D. H. Lawrence.* 8 vols. Cambridge: Cambridge University Press, 1979–(1993).

Britton, Derek. *Lady Chatterley: The Making of the Novel.* London: Unwin Hyman, 1988.

Coombes, Henry, ed. *D. H. Lawrence: A Critical Anthology.* Harmondsworth: Penguin, 1973.

Daleski, H. M. *The Forked Flame: A Study of D. H. Lawrence.* London: Faber, 1965.

Draper, Ronald P. *D. H. Lawrence: The Critical Heritage.* New York: Barnes & Noble, 1970.

Fernihough, Anne. *D. H. Lawrence: Aesthetics and Ideology.* Oxford: Clarendon Press, 1993.

Finney, Brian. *D. H. Lawrence: Sons and Lovers.* Harmondsworth: Penguin Books, 1990.

Ford, George H. *Double Measure: A Study of the Novels and Stories of D. H. Lawrence.* New York: Holt, Reinhart and Winston, 1965.

Fox, Elizabeth M. "Closure and Foreclosure in *The Rainbow.*" *The D. H. Lawrence Review* 27 no. 2–3 (1997–98): 197–215.

Gill, Stephen. "The Composite World: Two Versions of *Lady Chatterley's Lover.*" *Essays in Criticism* 21 (1971): 347–64.

Harvey, Geoffrey. *Sons and Lovers.* London: Macmillan, 1987.

Huxley, Aldous, ed. *The Letters of D. H. Lawrence.* London: Heinemann, 1932.

Ingersoll, Earl. *D. H. Lawrence, Desire, and Narrative.* Gainesville: University Press of Florida, 2001.

———. "Lawrence in the Tyrol: Psychic Geography in *Women in Love* and *Mr. Noon.*" *Forum for Modern Language Studies* 26, no. 1 (1990): 1–12.

Ingram, Allan. *The Language of D. H. Lawrence.* London: Macmillan, 1990.

Jackson, Dennis and Fleda Brown Jackson, eds. *Critical Essays on D. H. Lawrence.* Boston: G. K. Hall, 1998.

Kermode, Frank. *D. H. Lawrence.* New York: Viking Press, 1973.

Lewiecki-Wilson, Cynthia. *Writing Against the Family: Gender in Lawrence and Joyce.* Carbondale: Southern Illinois University Press, 1994.

Maddox, Brenda. *The Married Man: A Life of D. H. Lawrence.* London: Sinclair-Stevenson, 1994.

Mehl, Dieter and Christa Jansohn, eds. *The First and Second Lady Chatterley Novels.* Cambridge: Cambridge University Press, 1999.

Miko, Stephen, J. *Toward "Women in Love": The Emergence of a Lawrentian Aesthetic.* New Haven: Yale University Press, 1971.

Millet, Kate. *Sexual Politics.* London: Hart-Davis, 1971.

Moore, Harry T. *The Priest of Love: A Life of D. H. Lawrence.* London: Heinneman, 1974.

Nehls, Edward, ed. *D. H. Lawrence: A Composite Biography.* 3 vols. Madison: University of Wisconsin Press, 1957–59.

Nixon, Cornelia. *Lawrence's Leadership Politics and the Turn Against Women.* Stamford: University of California Press, 1986.

Oates, Joyce Carol. "Lawrence's *Götterdämerung:* The Tragic Vision of Women in Love." *Critical Inquiry* 4 (Spring 1978): 559–78.

Phillips, Gene D. "Ken Russell's Two Lawrence Films: *The Rainbow* and *Women in Love.*" *Literature/Film Quarterly* 25 no. 1 (1997): 68–73.

Poplawski, Paul. *D. H. Lawrence: A Reference Companion.* Westport: Greenwood, 1996.

Preston, Peter. *A D. H. Lawrence Chronology.* New York: St. Martin's Press, 1994.

Ross, Charles L. *The Composition of "The Rainbow" and "Women in Love": A History.* Charlottesville: University of Virginia Press, 1979.

———. "Editorial Principles in the Penguin and Cambridge Editions of *Women in Love.*" *The D. H. Lawrence Review* 21, no. 2 (Summer 1990): 223–6.

Ross, Charles L. and Dennis Jackson, eds. *Editing D. H. Lawrence: New Versions of a Modern Author.* Ann Arbor: The University of Michigan Press, 1995.

Ruderman, Judith. *D. H. Lawrence and the Devouring Mother: The Search for a Patriarchal Ideal of Leadership.* Durham: Duke University Press, 1984.

Sagar, Keith. *The Art of D. H. Lawrence.* Cambridge: The University Press, 1966.

———. *A D. H. Lawrence Handbook.* New York: Barnes & Noble Books, 1982.

Sanders, Scott. *D. H. Lawrence: The World of the Five Novels.* New York: Viking Press, 1973.

Smith, Anne, ed. *Lawrence and Women.* New York: Barnes & Noble Books, 1978.

Spika, Mark, ed. *D. H. Lawrence: A Collection of Critical Essays.* Englewood Cliffs: Prentice-Hall, 1963.

Squires, Michael. *The Creation of Lady Chatterley's Lover.* Baltimore: Johns Hopkins University Press, 1983.

———, ed. *D. H. Lawrence's Manuscripts: The Correspondence of Frieda Lawrence, Jake Zeitlin and Others.* London: MacMillan, 1991.

Squires, Michael and Dennis Jackson, eds. *D. H. Lawrence's "Lady": A New Look at "Lady Chatterley's Lover."* Athens: University of Georgia Press, 1985.

Whelan, P. T. *D. H. Lawrence: Myth and Metaphysic in "The Rainbow" and "Women in Love."* Ann Arbor: U.M.I. Research Press, 1988.

Widdowson, Peter, ed. *D. H. Lawrence.* London: Longman, 1992.

Worthen, John D. *D. H. Lawrence and the Idea of the Novel.* London: Macmillan, 1979.

———. *D. H. Lawrence.* London: Edward Arnold, 1991.

Index of Themes and Ideas

AARON'S ROD, 14, 84–85, 110–11, 112

CAPTAIN'S DOLL, THE, 117

FOX, THE, 117

KANGAROO, 12, 14, 117

LADY CHATTERLEY'S LOVER, 15, 85, 95–121; arrogance in, 106; and autobiography, 120–21; Mrs. Bolton in, 97, 98, 99, 100, 103; and Brontë sisters, 116–20; characters in, 102–3; Clifford Chatterley in, 95–96, 97, 98, 99, 100–101, 102, 106; Constance Chatterley in, 95, 96, 97–98, 99–101, 102, 106, 107, 108–9, 112, 115, 118; Sir Geoffrey Chatterley in, 95; Bertha Coutts in, 99, 100, 118; critical views on, 60, 104–21; Tommy Dukes in, 96, 97, 103, 109, 114–15; and enclosures in mansion *versus* expanse of woods, 96, 97, 98; Duncan Forbes in, 100; Arnold Hammond in, 109; Hilda in, 95, 97, 99–100, 101, 103, 106, 107, 108–9; and Lawrence as prophetic novelist, 12; Lawrence's letter to Morrison on distasteful content of, 104–5; and Lawrentian *daemonization* and *askesis,* 114–16; Sir Malcolm Reid in, 96, 100, 103; Oliver Mellors in, 95, 96, 97–98, 99–100, 101, 102–3, 106, 107, 108, 112, 115, 116; Michaelis in, 83, 96; nature imagery in, 99, 110–12; plot summary of, 95–101; as reflection of Lawrence's sad life, 112–14; sex and assault on verbal and visual consciousness in, 107–9; tenderness in, 105–6; titles of, 105–7; versions of, 95, 105–7, 118

LAWRENCE, D. H., biography of, 10, 13–15

LOST GIRL, THE, 14

"MOTHER AND DAUGHTER," 117

PLUMED SERPENT, THE, 12, 15, 117

RAINBOW, THE, 14, 41–65; biblical allusions in, 60–63; Anna Lensky Brangwen in, 41–42, 42–43, 44, 45, 46, 54, 56, 57–58, 62, 63, 64, 65; Gudrun Brangwen in, 44, 47; Lydia Lensky Brangwen in, 41, 42, 43, 44, 45, 46, 53, 56, 78, 80; Tom Brangwen in, 41, 42, 43, 44, 45, 46, 53–54, 56, 78, 80; Ursula Brangwen in, 11, 43, 44, 45, 46–47, 59, 62; William Brangwen in, 42–43, 44, 45, 46, 56, 57, 63, 64, 65; Cathedral scene in, 43, 55–58, 63–65; characters in, 46–47; critical views on, 9–12, 48–65,

78, 80; Expressionism and Cathedral scene in, 63–65; female superiority in natural sexuality in, 10–12; gaze in, 78, 80; and glorification of woman in order to punish her, 58–60; Winifred Inger in, 44; and Lawrence's letter to Lady Ottoline on libel suits, 48–49; nature scenes in, 110; plot summary of, 41–45; real-life relation between Lawrence and wife Frieda and women in, 52–55; Anton Skrebensky in, 11–12, 43, 44, 45, 47, 59, 78; Baron Skrebensky in, 43; and *Study of Thomas Hardy*, 55–58; and *them* (Oates), 50–52

SONS AND LOVERS, 13, 14, 15, 16–40; characters in, 21–22; critical views on, 9–12, 23–40; Baxter Dawes in, 18, 19, 20, 22; Clara Dawes in, 18, 19, 20, 22, 31–32, 35, 36, 49, 52; and destruction of Annie's doll, 39; and dialectic of space, 32–34; and disseminated consciousness, 29–32; Garnett's changes of, 27–32; images of women in, 38–40; labeling of Miriam Leivers in, 34–36; language and power of working class in, 36–38; and Lawrence's letter to Garnett on, 23–25; Leivers family in, 17, 18, 22; Miriam Leivers in, 13, 18–19, 20, 22, 27–28, 29, 31, 32, 33, 34–36, 53; library episode in Chapter VII in, 27–29; Annie Morel in, 17, 18, 20, 21, 39, 40; Arthur Morel in, 16, 17, 18, 19, 21–22; Gertrude Coppard Morel in, 16, 17–18, 19–20, 21, 23–24, 25–27, 30, 32–33, 37, 38, 39–40; Paul Morel in, 16, 17, 18–19, 20, 21, 23–24, 26, 27–28, 29, 30–32, 33, 35–36, 39, 40, 51, 53; Walter Morel in, 16, 17, 19, 21, 30, 37–38; William Morel in, 16, 17–18, 21, 23, 28; mother-blaming in, 25–27; plot summary of, 16–20; and Spencer, 28; Louisa Lily Denys Western ("Gyp") in, 17, 22

STUDY OF THOMAS HARDY, THE, 55–58

"TORTOISE SHOUT," 12

TRESPASSER, THE, 14

VIRGIN AND THE GYPSY, THE, 15

WHITE PEACOCK, THE, 13, 120–21

"WOMAN WHO RODE AWAY, THE," 117

WOMEN IN LOVE, 14, 66–94; ambivalence of lovers in, 9–10; Rupert Birkin in, 10, 66, 67, 68, 69, 70, 71, 72, 77, 78–79, 82, 83, 85, 88–90, 91–94, 112; Gudrun Brangwen in, 66, 67, 68, 69, 70, 71, 72, 75, 78, 79–82, 83, 87, 88, 89, 93; Ursula Brangwen in, 9–10, 66, 67, 68, 69, 70, 71, 72, 78, 79, 82, 83, 86–88, 89, 92–93, 112, 117; characters in, 72–73; Diana Crich in, 68; Gerald Crich in, 66, 67, 68, 69, 70, 71, 72, 75–77, 78, 80–82, 83, 85, 88–90, 93–94; Mr. Crich in, 68, 69, 70, 73, 75, 76;

Winifred Crich in, 68, 69, 73; critical views on, 74–94; death and rhetoric of representation in, 75–77; "Excurse" in, 9–10, 112; first version of, 91–94; gazes in, 77–82; good and evil in, 86–90; Julius Halliday in, 67, 70; innocence *versus* social being in, 86–90; and Lawrence as "prisoner of sex," 83–86; Lawrence's letter to Pinker on Lady Ottoline as model for Hermione in, 74; Loerke in, 71, 73, 82; nature imagery in, 110, 112; plot summary of, 66–71; psychology of void and center in, 82–83; The Pussum in, 67, 70, 73; Hermione Roddice in, 14, 66, 67–68, 69–70, 72–73, 74, 78

Wake Tech. Libraries
9101 Fayetteville Road
Raleigh, North Carolina 27603-5696

WAKE TECHNICAL COMMUNITY COLLEGE
3 3063 00133152 8

WN DATE DUE

JUL 2007